LECTIO DIVINA

Dear Karen,

Enjoy the variety of
prayer forms of lectio
divina. May these
possibilities gift you.

Lucy Wynkoop OSB

LECTIO DIVINA

CONTEMPLATIVE AWAKENING AND AWARENESS

Christine Valters Paintner
Lucy Wynkoop, OSB

Paulist Press
New York/Mahwah, NJ

Scripture extracts are taken from the *New Revised Standard Version, Catholic Edition* Copyright © 1993 and 1989, by the Division of Christian Education of the National Council of the Churches of Christ in the United States of America and reprinted by permission of the Publisher.

Cover design by Joy Taylor
Book design by Lynn Else

Library of Congress Cataloging-in-Publication Data

Paintner, Christine Valters.
    Lectio divina : contemplative awakening and awareness / Christine Valters Paintner, Lucy Wynkoop.
        p. cm.
    Includes bibliographical references.
    ISBN 978-0-8091-4531-7 (alk. paper)
    1. Bible—Devotional use. 2. Prayer—Christianity. 3. Spiritual life—Christianity. I. Wynkoop, Lucy. II. Title.
    BS617.8.P35 2008
    248.3—dc22

                                                                    2008029801

Published by Paulist Press
997 Macarthur Boulevard
Mahwah, New Jersey 07430

www.paulistpress.com

Printed and bound in the
United States of America

Contents

I dedicate my work on this book to the
loving memory of my mother (1942–2003).
—Christine Valters Paintner, OblSB

I am deeply grateful to the community of St. Placid Priory
for the way we treasure *lectio* as a formative piece
in our community living.
—Lucy Wynkoop, OSB

Preface

Lectio in Our Own Lives

Sr. Lucy Wynkoop, OSB:

Each of us began our relationship with *lectio divina* by responding to an invitation from God that helped us address our own hungers. I entered St. Placid Priory, a Benedictine monastery, in 1961. I rediscovered *lectio* while I was working on a master's in theology with a concentration in scripture and a master's in theology with a concentration in monastic studies. My love of scripture and my desire to pray with scripture confirmed for me that this ancient monastic practice was integral to my personal formation. In praying *lectio* with scripture, I learned that all of life can be *lectio*; God is always loving me and calling me to be more conscious of God's presence in every moment of my life.

As I worked with retreatants and directees, I began to understand how valuable a gift *lectio* could be for others. In my retreat work I developed ways to introduce *lectio divina* to participants. Retreatants were able to absorb and understand a more-structured approach to *lectio*. Eventually they were able to let the Holy Spirit pray in them *without* adhering to the structure. Dialogue provided opportunities for retreatants to share what was working in their depths. Participants bonded with one another as they shared insights from their *lectio*. The more I worked with retreatants, the more I hoped this gift could be more readily available for everyone. When Paul McMahon, managing editor at Paulist Press, suggested I write a book on *lectio divina*, I saw it as an opportunity to share the richness of the *lectio* experience with others.

Christine Valters Paintner, OblSB:

I initially discovered *lectio divina* while in graduate school. I began my studies with hardly any interest in the monastic way of life as I thought it had little to offer me. The more I studied and learned, however, the more I realized what deep wisdom the Benedictine way of balance and contemplation has to offer someone living in a modern world that values doing over being, speed over slowness, productivity over rest, and consumerism over simplicity. I realized that the Benedictine way of life was how I had been longing to pray and be in the world. The sense of surprise I felt over this discovery helped confirm for me that this was God's invitation.

What drew me so deeply into the practice of *lectio* was the way it reveals scripture as a living, dynamic text with multiple layers. Each layer can speak to us in different ways depending on what is happening in our life. The regular practice of *lectio* allows scripture to unfold again and again and shapes the way I listen to all of my experience. It is especially valuable in my ministry of spiritual direction, as a way of being with another person and listening for the movements of the Spirit. I began teaching and using *lectio divina* with my students, first in classes on prayer and Benedictine spirituality, and then in classes I was teaching on spirituality and the arts. In the latter case, the method of *lectio* was expanded to include praying with other "texts" such as poetry, music, visual art, and life experience, which we offer in a later chapter of the book.

Acknowledgments

We feel deeply privileged to have coauthored this book. Sister Lucy Wynkoop's Benedictine community at St. Placid Priory in Lacey, Washington, has helped shape and form her and fostered her love of *lectio divina*. Christine Paintner is profoundly grateful for the love and support of her husband John and for the care of her oblate community at St. Placid and its support in living the Benedictine life.

We would like to thank people who have gifted us with their time, wisdom, and scholarship in reading and commenting on our book. Karen Barrueto preedited our work. We are also grateful to Sister Teresa Jackson, OSB; Sister Teresa White, SP; John Forman, OblSB; Leah Cochran, OblSB; Roy DeLeon, OblSB; Sister Katherine Howard, OSB; Sister Maureen O'Larey, OSB; Sister Laura Swan, OSB; Sister Sharon McDonald, OSB; Sister Dorothy Robinson, OSB; Sister Monika Ellis, OSB; Sister Mary Giles Mailhot, OSB; and Father Benedict Auer, OSB. We also thank Kathryn Richert, Reverend Rosalind Ziccardi, Julie Barrett Ziegler, Noelle Rollins, Cheryl Eiger, Jerry DeVore, Diane Parker, Sue Luke, and Robyn Tsjuji.

In addition, we thank the following for granting us permission to use their material.

Original contributions—
Rosalind B. Ziccardi, "Example of *Lectio Divina* on Reading for Formation," "Example of *Lectio Divina* as Meditation," and "Example of *Lectio Divina* as Prayer." Used by permission of the author.

Noelle Rollins, "Practical Application of *Lectio* Using Rachel M. Srubas's poem 'Ready Me to Respond.'" Used by permission of the author.

Sr. Dorothy Robinson, OSB, "Another Simple Way to Pray *Lectio Divina*." Used by permission of the author.

Julie Barrett Ziegler, "Example of a Prayer Altar," "About Writing the Icons *Our Lady of Tenderness* and *Our Lady of Sorrows*," "Example of *Lectio Divina* with the Icons *Our Lady of Tenderness* and *Our Lady of Sorrows*," and "Example of *Motio Divina* in Doing a Wide Range of Motions." Used by permission of the author.

Cheryl K. Eiger, image used as an "Example of *Lectio Divina* on Romans 7:15 through Making Art." Used by permission of the artist.

Mary Giles Mailhot, OSB, "Example of *Lectio Divina* through Use of the Movie *Matilda*." Used by permission of the author.

Jerry R. DeVore, PhD, "Example of *Lectio Divina* through Use of the Music of Hildegard of Bingen." Used by permission of the author.

John Forman, haiku on page 112. Used by permission of the author.

Also—

Rachel M. Srubas, "Ready Me to Respond," from *Oblation: Meditation on St. Benedict's Rule*, by Rachel M. Srubas. Copyright © 2006 by Rachel M. Srubas. Used by permission of Paraclete Press, www.paracletepress.com.

Julie Ziegler Barrett, iconographer, the icons *Our Lady of Tenderness* and *Our Lady of Sorrows*, commissioned by St. Michael's Parish in Olympia, Washington, for their Chapel of Repose. Used by permission of the artist.

CHAPTER ONE

What Is Lectio Divina?

"If you continue in my word, you are truly my disciples."
—John 8:31

Lectio Divina as Invitation

Lectio divina means "holy or sacred reading." It is an ancient Christian prayer-form being rediscovered and reclaimed in our time. *Lectio* is a slow, contemplative praying of the scriptures, which leads us to union with God. It is an invitation to listen deeply for God's voice in scripture and then to allow what we hear to shape our way of being in the world.

By picking up a copy of this book you are responding to an invitation, one that originated with God's still, small voice within. This invitation may be a response to your hunger for some guidance on how to enter into a deeper relationship with the sacred texts that shape the Christian faith and way of life. Perhaps you are already familiar with *lectio divina* but seek tools that will bring you even deeper into the practice of this ancient form of prayer.

We wrote this book to help the beginner enter into an encounter with God through a contemplative way of being with holy scripture, and to help those more familiar with *lectio* to find ways in which it can invite them into a rhythm and way of being in the world.

A Brief History of *Lectio Divina*

The roots of *lectio* can be found in the Jewish synagogue where the *haga*, or meditation on the Hebrew Scriptures, is practiced by rabbis and their disciples: "To fix the sacred words in their minds and hearts they murmured them aloud like bees feeding on honey."[1] The fathers of the church expanded the concepts of reading and speaking the scriptures as prayer. In homiletics they sought the deeper or spiritual sense of the scriptures. Origen is given credit for coining the Greek term that in Latin is known as *lectio divina*.[2] The desert mothers and fathers believed that they heard God speaking to them, personally and immediately, through scripture. They saw scripture as a privileged place for encountering God. In the monasteries that were formed out of this desert experience and call, *lectio divina* became a central practice. Most monastics would not have been able to read the scriptures individually because books were very expensive at the time. They experienced the Word communally, in the liturgy and in the memorization of sacred texts. St. Pachomius stressed the fundamental need for all monastics to memorize the Psalter and the New Testament.[3] He emphasized the importance of recalling memorized texts so that they could bear fruit in one's life.

Out of this tradition of immersion in scripture, St. Benedict wrote his *Rule* (hereafter *RB*) early in the sixth century. He prescribes holy reading, *lectio divina*, as one of the central activities to occupy a monk's day: about three hours each day depending on the season, and more reading on Sunday (*RB* 48). This was in addition to the seven or eight offices the monks would have gathered together to pray daily (*RB* 8–19).

In the twelfth century, Guigo II, a Carthusian monk, wrote *The Ladder of Monks*, which uses the image of Jacob's ladder to systematize *lectio divina* into stages or steps of a process. Following an initial reading of a passage of scripture, the first step, called *lectio* ("reading"), was to allow a phrase or word to arise out of the text and to focus on it. The second step, called *meditatio* ("meditation"), was to ponder the word(s) of the sacred text. The spontaneous movement of the will in response to these reflections was the third step, known as *oratio* ("prayer"). The fourth step, *contemplatio* ("contemplation"), was the practice of resting in God's silence.[4] Later in this chapter we will flesh out these steps and invite the reader to begin praying.

Lectio and Formation

Lectio invites us to read for formation, not for information or entertainment value. Spiritual formation is the process of coming to know God and allowing God's vision and values to shape us. This is not just an intellectual exercise but one that involves the whole person: heart, body, and spirit. Knowing God in this way is an intimate, felt way of knowing.

The process of formation is initiated by God, but we can develop habits of prayer and other spiritual practices that can open us more deeply and consciously to God's work in us. Galatians 4:19 speaks of this: "My little children, for whom I am again in the pain of childbirth until Christ is formed in you." We are formed; we ourselves do not do the forming. However, we can choose whether to support the formation process or hinder it. We can choose openness, cooperation, and cocreation with God as ways to enhance the process of entering into the full image and likeness of Christ, and of expressing the truth of who we are. *Lectio divina* is one way to choose a stance of openness and cooperation with God's formative work in us.

Reading for formation, rather than information, requires a radical posture of deep listening. In the *Rule of Benedict* we are invited to listen deeply with "the ear of [our] heart" to the voice of God in scripture (Prologue v. 1, 10). This kind of listening takes practice and patience since it is not our normal way of being in the world and with others. How easy it is to anticipate what we will say next rather than to listen with spiritual awareness to the story of another person. Being fully present is a valuable gift we can offer to the world.

Scripture is God's Word to us. *Lectio divina* invites us into a sacred relationship with the Word and nurtures in us a way of being with God that gradually spills over into the whole of our lives. When we nourish this deep listening to God in scripture, we slowly discover the voice and presence of God in our loved ones. Then, perhaps, we can offer this gift even to those who irritate us. Eventually, the whole of creation has the potential for opening us up to an encounter with God.

Lectio divina is so much more than a prayer technique. It is a way of cultivating a posture of receptivity to God in the whole of our experience. *Lectio* is reading for insight to encounter the living God, not to glean information. Through *lectio,* a friendship with the Holy One develops and a new way of life is born.

When we engage in *lectio divina,* we are essentially saying that we believe scripture has something unique to say to each one of us. It has wisdom to offer us in each moment of the spiritual journey. *Lectio divina* is reverential listening; it is listening in a spirit of silence and awe; it is a time for savoring God's Word and lingering in God's presence. It gives us an opportunity to attend to the still, small voice of God that speaks to us intimately and personally.

The Steps of *Lectio Divina*

The original monastic way of doing *lectio divina* was to listen to how God is addressing us through a particular text of scripture. From this perspective there are no stages, ladders, or steps. It is more like one organic process with four "moments"—reading, meditating, praying, and contemplating—flowing naturally into one another. Each is joined to the other in an interrelated pattern, and to the center where God speaks to the heart. To pay attention to any one of the four is to be in direct relationship with all the others. You may begin your prayer with any of them and move easily from one to another according to the inspiration of the Holy Spirit. If you pray this way often enough it will become so much a part of you that you will no longer need to be conscious of particular steps. Then *lectio divina* will become a holy rhythm; you will live and breathe and move with God.

For the sake of those in the early stages of this journey, we offer the following guidelines of preparation for the different stages of *lectio divina*. We will go into much greater depth for each stage in the chapters that follow.

Preparing for God's Word

You will need to choose a scripture passage with which to pray. Consider one of the daily readings of the Church, a gospel passage, or a psalm. If you meet regularly with a spiritual director you can ask for a suggestion. For practice, we invite you to pray with the following passage from Hosea:

> Therefore, I will now allure her, and bring her into the wilderness, and speak tenderly to her. From there I will give her vineyards, and make the Valley of Achor a door of hope. There she shall respond as in the days of her youth, as at the time when she came out of the land of Egypt. On that day, says the LORD, you will call me, "My husband" ....And I will take you for my wife forever; I will take you for my wife in righteousness and in justice, in steadfast love, and in mercy. I will take you for my wife in faithfulness; and you shall know the LORD. (Hos 2:14–16, 19–20)

Allow enough time to enter deeply into this experience. Plan at least a half hour of uninterrupted time at first. With practice you will come to know how much time is "enough." The heart of *lectio divina* is cultivating the ability to listen deeply, to hear "with the ear of your heart." The prophet Elijah listened for the still, small voice of God. The "sound of sheer silence" (1 Kgs 19:12) is God's word to you, God's gentle voice touching your heart. Deep listening is a process of attuning yourself to the presence of God. In order to hear this quiet voice you must learn to love silence. Our modern culture surrounds us with noise from the Internet, television, radio, video games, and constant conversation. It takes time to make a transition from the noise of the day to a place of inner stillness where we can listen intensely. Having a regular place and a specific time for *lectio* helps the transition from busyness to stillness. Use whatever method is best for you and allow yourself to enjoy silence.

Sit comfortably, and shift your body so you feel relaxed and open. Take as much time as you need to turn inward and settle into stillness. It is often helpful to notice your breathing: as you breathe in, be aware of the presence of the Spirit; as you breathe out, let go of all that distracts you from this time of prayer. Place any worries or burdens in God's care. You might notice a response of gratitude for the freely given gift of each breath. When you feel fully present and ready to listen to God's voice, begin.

Reading God's Word (Lectio)

Read the scripture passage at *least* twice, out loud slowly, the first time for familiarity, the second time to enter more deeply into the text. Savor each phrase and gather the words into your depths. Listen for a word or phrase that captures your attention. Notice what shimmers, beckons, invites, or speaks to you. Be open to what unnerves you, disturbs you, or stirs you. There may be a word that seems especially ripe with meaning at this time. Some days a phrase will jump right off the page; other days you will experience a more subtle and gentle invitation. Listen until you have a sense of which words are speaking to you and then repeat them to yourself in the silence. Savor this experience.

Reflecting on God's Word (Meditatio)

Read the scripture passage again and continue to savor each word or phrase that speaks to you. Allow the words to unfold in your imagination and work within you. Let them speak even more deeply. Notice what feelings or images arise for you. Allow the Spirit to expand your capacity for listening and to open you to a fuller experience of scripture. Begin to notice where this passage speaks to your life. What do you see, hear, touch, or remember? Let the text interact with your thoughts, hopes, memories, and desires. Rest in this experience for some time; God's Word is speaking to you in this moment.

Responding to God's Word (Oratio)

After a time, as your insight deepens, you will be moved to respond and say yes to God. When this happens, notice how the words relate to your life right now. How do they speak to what you have heard and seen this day? How do they connect with what is happening at home, at work, or in your leisure time? Take some time to explore how God is present to you and has called you to look at something in your circumstances. Is there a challenge being presented to you? Address your response to God in whatever way seems appropriate. You may be led to speak from your heart, write in a journal, or express yourself through some artistic medium or movement. Allow yourself to be as spontaneous as possible. Your whole being can become prayer through the honest expression of your deepest thoughts, feelings, and desires in dialogue with God. Give yourself permission to be touched and changed by the Word of God.

Resting with God's Word (Contemplatio)

Contemplation is a time for resting in the presence of the One who has spoken to you intimately and personally. Rest in the silence of God's loving embrace and allow your heart to be moved to gratitude for this time of prayer. Anyone who has ever been in love knows that there are instances when words are not necessary, instances beyond words where you simply delight in the presence of the beloved. Allow yourself to simply *be* in God's presence. Let go of words and practice silence. Cultivate receptivity; take in all that God offers you right now.

A Fifth Step: Becoming God's Word (Operatio)

The sometimes-added fifth step of *lectio* is called *operatio* or action. It is the moment when we end our prayer and return to daily life. This step or stage of the process includes all of our time until we next sit down again to our practice of *lectio divina*. *Operatio* is essentially about taking our prayer into our everyday lives and responding to our lives from that experience of prayer.

Following a structure in *lectio divina* helps guide people through the process. However, the danger of using a structure is that we can then get locked into expectations about the "right" way to pray and move into intimacy with God. Overanalyzing our practice can cause the spontaneity of the spiritual journey to get lost, and we make the *process* more important than the *journey* of prayer.

As you regularly pray scripture using *lectio divina,* you will encounter the transformative power of God's Word. One of the fruits of regular practice of *lectio* is that it becomes part of our way of being in the world. If you can hold the structure lightly, you will find yourself drawn into deeper levels of listening during your prayer time, rather than into stages of technique.

Four Senses of Scripture

The ancients identified four senses of scripture: literal, allegorical, moral, and unitive. These describe four levels of listening to the same passage. The ancients believed that scripture contains a mysterious dynamism that moves one to ever-deeper levels of understanding the Word of God.

Modern biblical scholars focus primarily on the literal sense of scripture. They seek out the historical and cultural background of the text and the meaning of particular words in order to enrich their interpretation. This way of looking at scripture is invaluable to better understand the meaning of the sacred texts.

While this kind of scholarship helps increase our understanding of the text, it is *not* the final goal of *lectio divina*. As we pray with scripture and interiorize its message, we move into the allegorical sense. We slowly begin to realize that the scriptures are about *us*; our life is reflected in its pages and the words have much wisdom to offer us. When we relate our own personal spiritual journey to the events in sacred texts, we are listening to the scriptures in a very different way. They are no longer just historical documents but stories about our own spiritual journey. For example the story of the Israelites' liberation from Egypt becomes the story of our own conversion. Geographical spaces like the desert come to symbolize interior places. The passage of the Israelites through the desert teaches us about letting go of attachments and moving more deeply into the embrace of God. The allegorical approach shows us how each scripture passage is a multifaceted message that speaks directly to our hearts and lives.

Out of an understanding of the personal relevance of scripture, we are moved to put words into practice in our lives. We come to understand scripture more by embodying it in our lives. When we begin to live by scripture, we are engaging the moral sense, allowing it to inform, expand, or shift our sense of what is right and good.

The moral sense leads us to the unitive level of scripture. This fourth level is reached when we are deeply immersed in God's Word. We have assimilated the sacred texts and they have become a part of us.

The four senses parallel the four stages of *lectio divina*. In both cases we are talking about a *spiral* journey, not a *linear* one; we return again and again to the same scripture passages. Through the prayer of *lectio*, the words take on new and deeper meaning with each return. As we experience the four senses, we are brought to another level of understanding of the text. All aspects of the contemplative life move in this deepening spiral. When we revisit sacred stories, we also revisit our limitations and wounds, but from another perspective because we have been changed. Gradually, as our friendship with God deepens, the four senses of scripture unfold as a dynamic part of our lives.

Overview of the Remaining Chapters

The chapters that follow invite us to a deeper experience of prayer through the movements of *lectio divina* and the senses of scripture. Each chapter will conclude with a list of some practical applications, and some chapters will have an example of applying the principles of the chapter. Chapter 2 will explore the idea of relational communication: what it means to listen deeply in all areas of our lives, and the ways we can prepare ourselves for our time of prayer. Chapter 3 will further explore the idea of reading for formation and the literal sense of scripture. Chapter 4 will focus on meditation and the allegorical or christological sense of scripture. Chapter 5 will explore the moral, or behavioral, sense of scripture and the prayerful response to sacred text. Chapter 6 will center on contemplation and how the unitive sense of scripture invites us to *be* with newfound insights. Chapter 7 will provide an explanation of how *lectio divina* can be both study and prayer. Chapter 8 is geared for those who need spiritual nourishment but have limited time to do *lectio*. Additional texts are offered for *lectio*. Chapter 9 will suggest some ways to write and use art in response to *lectio* as well as pray with art using *lectio*. Chapter 10 will conclude the book with a look at how to extend *lectio divina* beyond a way of being with scripture, to a way of being with God and life. It will show how we can become "heart people" through the principles of Michael Casey's "Prayer of the Heart"[5] which he derives from Benedict's *Rule*. This leads us into action. In the appendix we offer a summary of the practical steps for beginning *lectio divina,* as well as a bibliography and further readings to guide you.

We encourage you to take a moment to relish the invitation that has brought you this far in your reading, an invitation that is a response to your desire to know God in a loving and personal way through the words of sacred scripture. May the chapters that follow nourish you as you respond to the hunger in your heart and God's call.

Practical Applications

- Select a regular place for daily *lectio* that is free from distractions.
- Create this space with the intention of using it regularly as a sort of "transforming" or "transporting" place for yourself. This reading/listening/thinking/praying space will be as unique as you are. Pay attention to what helps *you*, personally, to enter a quiet, inward kind of reflective, *receptive* mood. Do you wish to have certain colors present? A candle? Images of personal experience or Divinity? Remember that your environment can either help or hinder the activity that occurs within it. This space can be as simple as a chair and a nearby candle, or an entire room designated for prayer and meditation. Creating a prayer space for *lectio* can be a first step in your intention to creating a deeper contemplative practice. This can be a sacred act, a gift for your inner life.
- Choose a short scripture passage, about a paragraph long, preferably from the Gospels, daily readings of the Church, or the psalms.

Example of a Prayer Altar
by Julie Barrett Ziegler

In one of the many "altar" spaces in my home, I have created a quiet place for *lectio* in front of a small, high desk with a little shelf on the top. A beautifully framed prayer quote from Fra Giovanni (c. 1513) hangs above this shelf. I read it aloud every morning. Beside the prayer stands a beloved Wayang Golek hand puppet, which speaks of beauty and purpose to me; she comes alive only through my own intention. A singing bowl and a sculpture of a hand in a mudra position (a sacred gesture in Buddhism) that holds my rosary complete this altar space. I receive peace just standing before these images and they invite me into morning praise every day.

For the years I was a single parent, in a tiny house with small children, the windowsill over my kitchen sink was my prayer altar. On the sill were a few family photos, a small votive candle, small elements from nature, a special stone from one of our daily walks, a revolving selection of postcard-sized sacred images, and a beloved saying I still use to this day, for my own strengthening:

Fall into the Mystery placed before you—
the one you will become will catch you.

I still think of that windowsill altar during challenging times and feel its empowering effect, even after all these years.

CHAPTER TWO

Deep Listening

Listen with the ear of your heart.
—*Rule of St. Benedict*, Prologue 1

In this chapter we explore what it means to listen deeply for God's Word to us. Listening is the foundation that supports each step of praying *lectio divina*. To listen deeply, there needs to be silence and space. We live in a culture that continuously offers us distractions; we are flooded with information on a daily basis; silence is constantly being filled with sound. Reflect for a moment on your day and notice all of the times you felt drawn to turn on the television or the radio or the computer. This continuous background noise in our lives makes it challenging to listen well, so there is much competing for our attention. *Lectio divina* is an invitation to become more intentional about the sounds we fill our lives with and the space we make for God's voice to reverberate in the stillness of our hearts.

God Is Communication

The very first line of John's Gospel tells us, "In the beginning was the Word, and the Word was with God, and the Word was God." God is *Word* to us, a source of powerful communication inviting us into a deeper relationship. To hear God's Word, listening must involve the whole person. In deep listening we open our hearts, minds, and souls to whatever God is offering us at this particular time in our lives. The gifts offered to us through the practice of inner listening have the potential to awe us and form us in profound ways.

In our commitment to *lectio divina* as a transformative prayer, we begin with the fundamental assumption that God wants to continuously speak to our hearts through scripture in a special and intimate way. Scripture is rife with meaning. The principle undergirding *lectio divina* is that God inspires each word that appears in the text, and that God continues to speak through that word. *Lectio divina* offers us a dynamic experience of a God who continues to communicate in the most intimate and personal ways directly to our hearts in the midst of our concrete life circumstances. Listening taps into our hunger for an authentic experience of God.

The Listening That We Are

We may or may not be aware of the expectations we bring to our reading of scripture. We also read it with a lens (or lenses) shaped by our culture, gender, class, and personal history. Everything that has been a part of our lives since the moment of our creation has had a role in shaping how we listen and what we expect to hear. The regular practice of *lectio divina* cultivates in us the ability to listen in a more intentional way. We become the listeners we were created to be. There is a contemporary story that illustrates this well:

Once two friends were walking down the sidewalk of a busy city street during rush hour. There were all sorts of noise in the city; car horns honking, feet shuffling, people talking! And amid all this noise, one of the friends turned to the other and said, "I hear a cricket."

"No way," her friend responded. "How could you hear a cricket with all of this noise? You must be imagining it. Besides I've never seen a cricket in the city."

"No really, I do hear a cricket. I'll show you." She stopped for a moment, then led her friend across the street to a big cement planter with a tree in it. Pushing back the leaves she found a little brown cricket.

"That's amazing!" said her friend. "You must have super-human hearing. What's your secret?"

"No, my hearing is just the same as yours. There's no secret," the first woman replied. "Watch, I'll show you." She reached into her pocket, pulled out some loose change, and threw it on the sidewalk. Amid all of the noise of the city, everyone within thirty feet turned their head to see where the sound of the money was coming from.

"See," she said. "It's all a matter of what you are listening for."[1]

What are *you* listening for in your life? In the Emmaus story found in Luke 24, the disciples walk along the road with Jesus but do not recognize him. They are not listening for him. When we approach scripture, especially a story we have heard many times before, are we open to the unexpected? Or do we have an expectation of how this story "should" affect us? Do we make an assumption before we read the text about how we should be shaped by it? What we listen for clearly influences what we are able to hear. As we listen to God speak, we are called to be aware of our own patterns of resistance.

Assumptions often happen in our human conversation as well. Before friends finish telling us their stories, we are constructing a response in our thoughts: we are not listening fully, but waiting for our turn to speak. When we are not fully present to them, we close off the possibility that there is something new to be heard or discovered.

Human beings have a fundamental need to be in relationships. We were created to be in community with others and with all of creation. Communication is an essential aspect of relationship. There will always be limitations to our listening: the expectations we bring, the way we are feeling on a particular day, the hopes and disappointments we carry. When we are unaware of this, however, our listening remains closed off from the fullness of possibility. *Lectio divina* invites us to become aware, to be the listeners we were created to be, and to listen for the sounds of God speaking to us in new ways.

Listening with Humility and Openness

The word *humility* is derived from the Latin word *humus,* which means "earth." Humility means being grounded in our earthiness and connected to the truth of who we are. The medieval monastic theologian St. Bernard of Clairvaux talked about Benedict's concept of humility as a means of getting in touch with the whole truth of who we are with our limitations and our strengths.[2] When practicing humility, we acknowledge that God is always far greater than we are and that God's imagination surpasses our ability to imagine. We acknowledge that each of us is uniquely gifted and finite. We are not called to be everything to everyone. We are called to be simply our authentic selves.[3] When we recognize this truth we can begin to approach God and sacred scripture with awe. We will be able to hear how God is speaking to our unique abilities and circumstances. We will be able to listen for the ways God is calling us to say both yes and no.

When we listen intently to scripture, we do not know what will happen in that divine encounter. Conversation and conversion both come from the same Latin root. The Latin *conversare* means "to turn around." In the *Rule of St. Benedict,* the word *conversatio* is used to describe the essential rhythm of monastic life. The monastic is turned around again and again by God working through community, scripture, liturgy, and life events. Conversion is a commitment to falling more and more in love with God. It is a practice of being open to the new ways that God is speaking to us and the ways that God is inviting us to something new. This practice of *lectio divina* challenges us to let go of our agendas and make room for God to surprise us with our truth and the truth of others. Can we lay aside our assumptions and expectations to listen with new ears and see with new eyes? Can we read scripture and allow ourselves to be transformed?

Listen with the Ear of Your Heart

The very first words of St. Benedict's monastic *Rule* are an invitation to "listen with the ear of your heart" (Prologue 1). The ear of the heart listens for the voice of God above all of the other voices competing for our attention. Listening is "taking in." We gather the Word into the very depths of our being. The meaning of the Hebrew word *heart (leb)* includes the heart and the soul of the human being. The word *heart* does not simply refer to a physical organ or the seat of our emotions. It also includes other layers of meaning, such as inner understanding, feelings, will, desire, conscience, and the seat of courage. The heart is an organ that represents the very core of our being. When we listen with the ear of the heart, we listen for God to break through to the innermost chamber, the very center of our being where there are no separate categories of sacred and secular. Listening with the ear of the heart enables us to enter into relationship with God through all aspects of our lives. What are we saying yes and no to in order to deepen our relationship with God? How does our listening move us to greater love?

Throughout scripture, God challenges us to have hearts of flesh rather than stone. In Psalm 95, the psalmist cries out, "O that today you would listen to [God's] voice! Do not harden your hearts" (Ps 95:7–8). A heart of flesh is open, vulnerable, permeable, and malleable in God's hands. It is a humble heart that is open to being surprised by God. We are invited to a place of gentleness with ourselves and others where we do not need walls around the wounds and cracks, which God can touch and heal. The ear of the heart is willing to surrender those narrow perspectives that are not large enough for God's mystery. The heart is the place of our most profound conversion.

Speech, especially in the Hebrew Scriptures, is the medium of divine self-disclosure. Therefore the fundamental stance of the person of faith is to listen. We hear this in the Shema, the great confession recited daily by Catholics in the Liturgy of the Hours at compline and by our Jewish brothers and sisters: "Hear, O

Israel: The Lord is our God, the Lord alone" (Deut 6:4). The Hebrew word *dabar* means not only "speech," but also "event" or "circumstance." Therefore, in the tradition of scripture, the Word speaks and acts. It becomes a part of our experience. We listen and we live the Word.

The prophet Isaiah describes God as the one who "morning by morning…wakens my ear to listen as those who are taught" (Isa 50:4). In Isaiah 55:3, God asks us to incline our ears and come: "listen, so that you may live." Deep listening is *always* a creative and life-giving act. The Word does not offer us just information that we can analyze and categorize. It is a living word that encourages us to extend our boundaries. God's Word is always larger than we are.

The Practice of Listening

The term *spiritual practice* has become more popular in recent years. The notion of practice implies a regular commitment to something so that it can take root in our hearts, shape us, and become a part of who we are and how we live in the world. When we practice listening, we become more and more aware of the internal and external things that distract us. We become intentional about listening for God's voice in the midst of all the other voices in our lives. We choose to lift God's voice up and allow it to shape our understanding and our hopes. We create time and space to cultivate the practice of deep listening.

A central aspect of the practice of listening is to set aside our expectations and assumptions as much as possible. Then we can see the potential in each moment for something new to be revealed. To pray through listening deeply is to be present in a deliberate and humble way to whatever God is doing deep within us. Learning to listen well takes time and teaches us patience.

Lectio divina is about developing a relationship with God. We listen with the "ear of our heart" for the God who is ever-active and who always calls us into a deeper relationship. God calls us to our true selves and asks the very ground of our being to respond. When we listen with our heart, we listen with love that is rooted in gratitude and appreciation. Everyone and everything speaks to us of God.

Silence, Stillness, and Solitude

Psalm 46 tells us to "Be still, and know that I am God!" (Ps 46:10) The Christian tradition is filled with great wisdom about the need for silence, stillness, and solitude in our lives. Stillness can renew and refresh us because for a few moments we are able to release our compulsive *doing*. Our culture tells us we are valuable when we perform, produce, or achieve. God tells us we are valuable as we *are*.

We may turn off the phone, television, computer, and radio and settle into the silence—only to become aware of the enormous volume of internal chatter that flows through our minds. Regular practice helps us to be still. Instead of berating ourselves for being so easily distracted when we pray, we can learn to treat ourselves gently. We can simply notice the thoughts as they rise up and then release them to God's care.

Solitude focuses on *presence*. A heart listening to a heart and attending to love provides us with opportunity for self-discovery, reflection, and inner peace. What resides in our hearts quiets us and provides a calmness so we can connect with ourselves, God's Word, and others. If we can internalize the Word within us, we can connect it with whatever surrounds our lives.

Preparing for *Lectio Divina*

Creating a regular rhythm of praying and listening can help you become more and more receptive to God's Word. It may take time to recognize how much time is "enough," but at the beginning, try to set aside a half hour of uninterrupted time.

It is often helpful to create a transition ritual to mark a time of silence and prayer. Lighting a candle can signal your intention of making the time sacred and special. Creating a small altar with a symbol of the presence of the sacred, such as a cross, icon, or statue, can also help to focus your attention.

Come as you are in *this* moment to *lectio divina,* and bring the fullness of your experiences and hopes. Become aware of how your body feels. Notice if there are any places of discomfort and shift your body if you need to. Relax into your posture. You might want to put your hands in an open and receptive posture to indicate your readiness to listen to God. Get in touch with your breathing. Pray to the Holy Spirit to enlighten and inspire you. The Latin root of the word *inspiration* means "to breathe in." As you breathe in, become aware of how the Spirit fills you. Let this awareness bring you into God's presence. Let God's presence inspire you with the breath of new life.

Even if you were to spend your whole time of prayer just slowing down, becoming still, resting in silence, and relishing the solitude—that is enough. You might want to just practice slowing down for several days at first. Try to set aside all of your expectations except for one; expect to encounter God.

Summary

Listening is at the heart of *lectio divina.* Through listening we are invited to soften our hearts and meet the God who communicates with us through the scriptures. It takes time, as well as a sense of humility and openness, to practice this kind of deep listening. Settling down into prayer and learning to be still and present is how we prepare to receive God's Word. Be patient and offer this time to yourself and God as a gift.

Practical Applications

- Dedicate a specific time for *lectio* that will work best for you in your daily schedule. Mark it down in your calendar.

Begin with a brief period and add time if your schedule will allow. Twenty or thirty minutes is a good amount of time. Commit to this time every day if possible.

- Light a candle, and perhaps some liturgical incense, too.
- Relax your body by being aware of your body sensations. Close your eyes. Be aware and relax your head...your neck...your shoulders...your back...your right hand...your left hand...your right thigh...your left thigh...your right leg...your left leg...your right foot...your left foot...Keep moving your attention every few seconds to different parts of your body, especially the places that are tense.
- Notice your breathing. As you breathe in, be aware of the presence of the Spirit filling you; as you breathe out, let go of all that distracts you from this time of prayer.
- Listen with new ears and see with new eyes, with a spirit of openness to the unexpected. Listen and look with love.
- Set aside expectations and assumptions if you can.
- Open your hands to receive.
- Maintain a good, comfortable posture.
- Move into *lectio*, but only when you feel fully present and ready to listen to God's voice.

CHAPTER THREE

Reading for Formation

Strive in every way to devote yourself constantly to the
sacred reading so that continuous meditation will seep into
your soul and, as it were, will shape it to its image.
Somehow it will form that "ark" of the Scriptures.[1]
—John Cassian, *Conferences* 14:10

The Meaning of *Lectio*

Lectio literally means "reading." It is the name given by the
medieval monk Guigo to the first step in *lectio divina* using the ladder analogy.[2] In the first "moment" or step you will read the text
you have selected—but not in your usual way of reading. Most
of the reading we do in everyday life is for information, such as
e-mails, newspapers, and advertisements, or for entertainment,
such as magazines and novels. There are even speed-reading techniques to get information faster and to digest more information in
less time. In *lectio* we do not speed-read to get through the text to
the end. We read to allow the text to sink into our bodies and to
touch our hearts and souls. We savor the poetry of the language.
We relish the beauty of the moment we have carved out to listen
for God.

Lexicographer Egidio Forcellini identified three levels of reading: "(1) strictly speaking it means to collect; (2) in a deeper or
pregnant sense it means to select what one desires or needs out of
a plurality; and (3) to collect with the eyes, especially to run over
a written text with the eyes, gathering into oneself what is there."[3]
When we first read a text we are faced with a multitude of words.

The pregnant sense of reading is when we "select" the words that speak to our desires and needs. This describes an active relationship with God's Word, not a passive one. When we engage the text intentionally, it can give birth to new insights and possibilities in our lives. Finally, as we gather the wisdom of scripture in, it becomes knit into the very fabric of our being.

To do this kind of reading we need to be empty. Benedict uses the Latin verb *vacare*, which means "to be empty," eight times in chapter 48 of his *Rule*.[4] He encouraged this kind of spaciousness and freedom for *lectio*. While the rest of our lives may be filled with clutter and unending lists of things to do, *lectio* gives us an opportunity to enter fully into the time and space of prayer and to move toward greater inner freedom. The practice of *lectio* cultivates freedom for holiness, leisure, and blessing, and for freedom from compulsive busyness and clutter.

Benedictine sister Macrina Wiederkehr writes about what *lectio* means to her: "*Lectio* offers us a new way to read. Read with a vulnerable heart. Expect to be blessed in the reading. Read as one awake, one waiting for the beloved. Read with reverence."[5] In the act of emptying ourselves, we make space for blessing. In fact, we can expect to be blessed in our prayer if we come with a receptive heart. In the Gospels, Jesus tells the parable of the sower and the seed. The seed that falls on fertile, rich ground takes root and produces fruit a hundredfold (Matt 13:1–13). We are invited to read the scripture with hearts that are vulnerable; our hearts can be the fertile ground where God can sow blessings. When we are receptive in this way, when we allow the Word to happen to us, we will receive the blessing of the Word. God is able to work the earth of our hearts and form us: we needn't try to do this through our own efforts.

The Practice of *Lectio Divina*: The First Step—Reading God's Word

Our last chapter was about listening and preparing to hear the text. Now we invite you to take what you have learned and apply it to your time of *lectio*. Again, use the scripture text we suggested earlier:

> Therefore, I will now allure her, and bring her into the wilderness, and speak tenderly to her. From there I will give her her vineyards, and make the Valley of Achor a door of hope. There she shall respond as in the days of her youth, as at the time when she came out of the land of Egypt. On that day, says the LORD, you will call me, "My husband"....And I will take you for my wife forever; I will take you for my wife in righteousness and in justice, in steadfast love, and in mercy. I will take you for my wife in faithfulness; and you shall know the LORD. (Hos 2:14–16, 19–20)

Take a moment to remember you are in God's presence. Ask intentionally for a receptive heart to receive God's Word for you. Read the text selected at least once aloud, and then repeat it more slowly until you are stopped by a word or phrase that speaks to you. Listen for the word that seems to shimmer, beckon, unnerve, or challenge you. You are listening for God's voice in the sacred text. How do you know that it is God's voice? You may not know exactly *why* it is speaking to you, but it's important to trust your inner voice, the one that originates with God and connects you with the Holy Presence within.

Repeat the word or phrase to yourself, savor it, relish the sound and sense, and slowly let it work itself into the fertile ground of your heart. Draw the text inside of you and let the word drop from your mind down to your heart. Let go of the need to analyze and let God's Word take hold of you, shape you, and change you. This is a transformational path. Pray to see with God's eyes the truth that you need for this moment in your life. God's gaze will guide you and reveal what you most need for your healing and wholeness right now.

Lectio is *not* meant to be a conceptual exercise but an encounter with the living God who dwells within each person and within the text. The prayer of *lectio* is where these divine impulses meet and spark; it is a moment of revelation that speaks to where we are in our lives at this moment in time. We read to be united with God through Christ in prayer. This kind of reading is meant to engage us completely. It is done very *slowly* and *reflectively*, and is motivated by a longing to be touched by God, to be healed, and to be moved toward wholeness.

Lectio divina emphasizes the *quality* of the experience, not the *quantity* of text. The focus of the first step is on reading the text slowly, listening for the word or phrase that is calling to you, trusting that call, sitting with the word that is speaking to you, and letting it begin to touch your heart.

Lectio as an Embodied Act

We highly recommend reading the text aloud when doing *lectio*. Vocalizing the words forces us to slow down and dwell on each phrase instead of skimming over the text to get to the end. When we proclaim the word out loud, we are marking its difference from other kinds of reading. Reading aloud helps us to avoid distractions since it takes more effort and concentration than just reading silently.

Reading aloud is an embodied act. When we vocalize words, our lips, eyes, and ears are engaged. Our throats and lungs are occupied as we sustain our breath and the sound of the words hum within us. Memories are evoked, the heart activated. When we slow down and say words out loud, something happens inside and the Word becomes more deeply a part of us. Scholar Jean Leclercq writes:

> In the Middle Ages, as in antiquity, they read usually, not as today, principally with the eyes, but with the lips, pronouncing what they saw, and with the ears, listening to the words pronounced, hearing what is called the "voices of the pages." It is a real acoustical reading; *legere* means at the same time *audire*. One understands only what one hears.[6]

When we read aloud, the "voice of the pages" is reflected in our own voice. Voice and word become one voice. As we hold the words and let them sink inside, we experience embodiment as well. Our heart begins to move with a greater awareness of the Spirit who is always present. We often live our lives out of our heads forgetting that we have bodies as well. God's call to us is always toward greater wholeness and that includes waking up to the whole of who we are, body and soul.

Lectio means reading a passage out loud, repeating it over and over again, forming each word lovingly with our lips, and hearing the sounds of the words and the poetry of the text. As we listen for the word that speaks, trust it, and vocalize it, our bodies can take it in. Then we will be an instrument of God's Word as it vibrates within us.

Distractions

While reading, you may find yourself becoming easily distracted. In the Buddhist tradition, distraction during meditative prayer is called "monkey mind": the mind that is always grasping at worries about the present, concerns about the future, or lists of things to do. When you sit down to pray, ask God to be with you and to guide you. If you notice that you have become distracted, gently draw your attention back to the text. Be *kind* to yourself when you notice that your mind is wandering. Sometimes anger at our tendency to be distracted becomes another distraction. You may need to gently but consistently draw yourself back to the slow meditative demands of *lectio*. *Lectio divina* teaches us a whole new way of being with God in scripture, a way that takes lots of time and patience to practice. Allow yourself to be fully human as you open to the blessing God is offering you.

Being with the Word

Several things might occur as you listen for the word. You may find yourself immediately drawn to something and sense a deep resonance with it, a sense that it is addressing you right now. You may feel awe at the fact that God is speaking to you so directly. Another possibility is that you might be drawn to something but then start to doubt whether it is really God's invitation or your own agenda at work. See if you can allow yourself to embrace what emerges and trust what is revealed. It is also quite possible that *nothing* will really attract you at all, in which case you can slowly read several lines of scripture and be with that, or just rest in the silence and not proceed any further at this time. Give yourself permission to receive whatever happens and to practice trusting your own sense of where God is leading you.

Lectio divina is meant to restore and uplift us—it is not meant to drag us down by feeding a negative inner voice: "The matter of sacred reading must be such that it can sustain in us a sense of reverence and submission. It must be such that we can safely suspend our critical faculties and freely lay bare our soul to be moved."[7] When you notice critical thoughts rising up, just notice them and gently let them go. Practice surrendering to the moment and trusting what is there.

Come to *lectio* just as you are, bringing the fullness of your life experience to prayer. Perhaps you are in the midst of sorrow, darkness, confusion, or transition—or perhaps you are filled with joy and confidence. The more you practice *lectio*, the more receptive you will be to the text and the more its wisdom will speak to your life situation.

Literal Level of the Text

In the first chapter we offered an overview of the four senses of scripture. The first sense, the *literal* level, can enrich and complement the first "moment" of *lectio*. The literal level means learning about the author as well as when and why the author wrote the text. This level can involve gathering information from tools of interpretation and analysis. The literal level also includes the historical-critical method of scripture study, which focuses on the historical and cultural background of the text as well as its purpose and the intended audience. All of this can be helpful preparation as long as we do not let the study of scripture as headwork take the place of *lectio* as "heartwork."[8]

We will continue to use the Hosea text as an example of how to work with the literal sense of scripture. The Book of Hosea reveals a very sensitive, emotional man, who could move quickly from anger and violence to deep tenderness. He has been called both priest and prophet. His prophecy centers on his own marriage to Gomer, which was a personal tragedy that profoundly influenced his teaching. In married life he endured extremely painful experiences which then shaped his prophetic vision. Gomer was a "recidivist adulteress" who became the symbol for unfaithful Israel. Just as Hosea could not renounce his wife even when she was unfaithful, so Yahweh could not renounce Israel when she was unfaithful in her commitment to the covenant. Hosea began the tradition of using marriage as a metaphor to describe the relationship between Yahweh and Israel. God chastises Israel for her unfaithfulness but remains faithful to her and long suffering. The unifying theme of Hosea is divine compassion and the love of God who will not abandon Israel.[9] As we gather information on the literal sense of the text we deepen our understanding of God's love.

A historical approach to the text tells us that the events in the Book of Hosea occurred during the reign of the Judean kings Uzziah, Jotham, Ahaz, Hezekiah, and Jeroboam II (Hos 1:1). The Book of Hosea addresses issues of covenant and the challenges of living in the Canaanite world during the second half of the eighth century before Christ. The *Anchor Bible Dictionary* gives us some cultural background for the text: "According to Hosea, the people consecrated themselves at Baal-peor, soon after they had made the covenant with YHWH (Hos 9:10; Num 25:1–18). They were brought by YHWH to the land which he had blessed, but they turned to the Canaanite gods instead, and attributed blessings and success to Baal (Hos 2:7, 10–11...)."[10] This shows that Yahweh's love is gratuitous. Yahweh leads the people into the desert in order to give them divine gifts. In spite of Israel's unfaithfulness, God woos her: "Therefore, I will now allure her, and bring her into the wilderness, and speak tenderly to her" (Hos 2:14). Yahweh's response to Israel's offenses is to espouse his bride with generous gifts of justice, righteousness, tenderness, and fidelity.[11] This story of God's actions in history illustrates God's profound love for Israel and shows us how deeply we also are loved.

Summary

Lectio begins our encounter with sacred scripture. Reading in *lectio divina* is very different from our usual ways of reading. We slow down and embody the text; we listen for the word or phrase that calls to us. We may want to use the literal sense of scripture to discover new facets of the text. In the next chapter we move from reading into meditation.

Practical Applications

- Read the text aloud at least once and then repeat it more slowly until you are stopped by a word or phrase that speaks to your heart.
- Practice surrendering to the moment.
- Embrace what emerges and trust what is revealed.
- Give yourself permission to receive whatever happens.
- Repeat the word or phrase to yourself, savor it, and relish the sound and sense.
- Bring your life experience to prayer.

Example of *Lectio Divina* on Reading for Formation *by Reverend Rosalind Ziccardi*

I will take you for my wife in righteousness and in justice, in steadfast love, and in mercy. I will take you for my wife in faithfulness; and you shall know the Lord. (Hos 2:19b–20)

While I make *lectio* a somewhat regular practice, I do find that coming to prayer this way means specifically choosing to approach scripture with a heart open to a spiritual nudge that is different than I experience in my daily quiet time. So it was on January 17, 2007. Once I was in my regular "prayer chair," I quieted myself with breathing—seeking the Spirit as I breathed in, expelling the noise or distractions and concerns with every breath exhaled. Five times I consciously inhaled, feeling the air enter through my nose, down my windpipe, and into my lungs, and consciously exhaled, feeling the release of tension stored in my muscles and frame.

Once centered, I opened to a predetermined text, Hosea 2:14–23. I read the passage aloud, just to reintroduce myself to the text and the theme since I hadn't read Hosea in a long time. I read it again aloud, more slowly. I paused and was quiet, simply looking at the passage, and then I read it again more quietly, but still out loud. The words formed a picture in my mind and I found myself drawn to the image of God marrying Israel which, I realized, I had personalized: God willingly seeks and actively desires to be in intimate, direct, loving, tender relationship—not as words, not as concept, not as principle, but in a personal, familiar, connected way.

CHAPTER FOUR

Savoring the Word

In your cell, pluck the various kinds, fruits of the Scriptures—
make use of these delights—never let the Book depart from your
hands or your eyes—learn the psalter "word for word." [1]
—Saint Jerome

The next step in the *lectio divina* process is *meditatio,* "meditation." There are many methods and forms of meditation. Here we
introduce meditation in the *lectio divina* sense. After we sit with
scripture and listen for the word or phrase that invites us, we then
move into the second "moment," *meditatio,* where we move more
deeply into prayer and let it interact with our memories, feelings,
and images.

How the Ancients Meditated

Repetition was an integral part of meditation for the ancients.
This is one way to cultivate the connection between the word and
the heart. The ancient monks used the idea of rumination to
describe the process of meditation. Livestock chew in two steps
and digest through multiple stomach chambers. Rumination is the
slow and careful chewing of food that needs to be broken down
for the animal to assimilate it. This expressive word became a
metaphor for the way we can relate to God's Word. *Lectio divina*
is described as spiritual nourishment. When we ruminate on the
Word, it becomes part of the very fabric of our being. Most of us
do not live in regular contact with livestock. Sadly, with so much
emphasis on fast food and convenience, we have lost the sense of

what it means to chew food slowly and savor it. In Tanzania, the Benedictine community likens this process to chewing sugar cane. It takes time and effort to extract the sweetness. To meditate is to give our full attention to the word or phrase we are repeating, to chew it slowly, and to allow the full depth of meaning to resonate within and become part of us.

Because copies of the biblical texts were expensive and rare in ancient times, monastics had to memorize scripture in order to pray with it throughout the day. This practice of memorization embedded the texts in their minds and hearts. Reading the text aloud, as we explored in the last chapter, and also memorizing scripture enriched the monastics' practice of meditation. This made their relationship with the text an intimate encounter; the Word literally dwelled within them. Benedictine sister Dolores Dowling says that in ancient practice, to meditate was essentially "to prepare oneself by thinking it over, fixing it in the memory, learning it…by heart. Our monastic forebears would call it 'learning by mouth,' since the mouth mediates wisdom."[2]

Up until the twelfth century the reader would pronounce the words of scripture with the lips, and in this way hear the sentence seen by the eyes. The result is a "muscle memory" of the words spoken and an aural memory of the words heard. When we give our total attention to the text, memorize it with the mind and heart, and repeat it with the mouth and voice, the Word is then inscribed in our body and soul.

The Lost Art of Savoring

The word *savor* comes from the Latin *saporem* meaning "to taste." Savoring involves all of the senses. The word is also related etymologically to *sapientia,* meaning "wisdom." Slowing down and relishing God's creation with our senses leads us to a wisdom not found when we speed through our lives. Our consumer-driven culture encourages us to find happiness through buying, owning, and collecting. The drive is toward purchasing something new rather than enjoying what is there for us in the moment. We are told to speed up rather than slow down, to *do* rather than *be*, to extract profit rather than ponder meaning.

Tasting is about slowing down, lingering, and enjoying. The God of scripture invites us to revel in the gifts that savoring can offer. Psalm 34, a psalm of praise, invites us to "taste and see that [God] is good" (v. 8). In Mark's Gospel (14:3–8) the woman with the alabaster jar of expensive perfumed oil breaks it open and pours it on Jesus' head. The disciples are angered at this costly waste but Jesus rebukes them: "She has performed a good service for me" (v. 6). She knew that he would not be with them much longer, and in this act, both of them were savoring the time they had together through a celebration of the senses.

The Song of Solomon also invites us to more deeply attend to the world around us. The lover delights in the beauty of his beloved and enjoys the senses she evokes: "Your channel is an orchard of pomegranates with all choicest fruits, henna with nard, nard and saffron, calamus and cinnamon, with all trees of frankincense, myrrh and aloes, with all chief spices—a garden fountain, a well of living water, and flowing streams from Lebanon" (Song 4:13–15). The Christian tradition has often been suspicious of the delights of the senses. Yet if we believe in the incarnational nature of God's revelation—Christ coming down to earth and becoming flesh—we see that matter reveals itself as holy to us. The sacraments can lead us to an intimate experience of God that is rooted in the things of this world. God invites us to take time to celebrate the gifts of a material world.

Fred Bryant, a social psychologist at Loyola University, writes that savoring requires "attentive and appreciative awareness" of the present moment.[3] His research reveals that we savor in four dimensions: basking (receiving praise), thanksgiving (expressing gratitude), marveling (losing oneself in wonder and awe), and luxuriating (indulging one's senses). He writes that like any skill, we get better at it with practice.[4] Meditation gives us an opportunity to practice enjoying God's presence, marveling at God's goodness, and appreciating the gifts God offers us in scripture. We can learn to slow down and relish the delights offered to us in the Word and in creation.

The Practice of *Lectio Divina*: The Second Step— Meditating on God's Word

As described in the previous chapter, the first step involves reading the scripture text until it touches you in some way. You read until a word or phrase catches your attention. After spending a few moments resting with the text, you are ready to let it work in your heart more deeply. The second step of *lectio divina* begins when your heart is touched, then you stop reading and begin to meditate.

Return to the beginning of the text and read through it again until you reach the place where you were moved. Now allow the words to stir images, feelings, and memories. Trust what is being stirred within you. Be open to the way the word is working in your heart. Notice what new questions emerge, what insights and challenges unfold. Sometimes you will begin to see the word or phrase with new eyes, a sign that transformation is happening. *Meditatio* is *not* a process of analyzing or thinking about the words of the text, but rather a way of *being* with all that is stirred within you. It is the act of moving into relationship with the scripture passage. Lowering our resistance opens us to greater gratitude for whatever God is giving in the moment.

Dolores Dowling quotes Cistercian scholar Andre Louf: "If in the course of my reading, I have been struck by some saying, my heart has been wounded. I cannot cast the Word off. I stand guard over it, repeat it slowly in the silence of my heart. Then I yield up this Word of God to the spirit within me. Then my heart gives birth to prayer."[5] "Wounding of the heart" is a description of the very personal and often immediate way scripture can work within us by shaking us and challenging us. Jacob wrestled with the angel and in the process was both wounded and transformed (Gen 32:22–32). Meditation can often highlight something out of joint in our lives, wound our sense of who we are, and then bring us back into alignment with a new understanding. Scripture meets us with this challenge and invites us to change.

In the process of savoring the words that have captured our attention, we are drawn into a process of reminiscence. As we repeat the word it can stir a memory and spontaneously evoke a whole chain reaction of associations. Each word can act like a spark, igniting images and thoughts, inspiring connections to other scripture passages, and evoking memories, lines of poetry, or words of a song. When we meditate, we make space for all of the connections that unfold for us. Macrina Wiederkehr describes the process of meditation beautifully:

> A touched heart means God has, in some way, come. God has entered that heart. Begin your meditation. Meditation is a process in which you struggle with the Word of God that has entered your heart. If this Word wants to be a guest in your heart, go forth to meet it. Welcome it in and try to understand it. Walk with it. Wrestle with it. Ask it questions. Tell it stories about yourself. Allow it to nourish you. Receive its blessing. To do this you must sink your heart into it as you would sink your teeth into food. You must chew it with your heart.[6]

As we meditate on the text, it works on us and we can trust that whatever rises up within us is precisely what we need to hear.

As you meditate, a word or image will enter your heart and demand your attention. Struggle with it. Create space for it. Reflect on it. Repeat it and memorize it so that it is available to you throughout the day. Consider it from different perspectives. Be aware of God's presence. Allow the senses to evoke images and reveal new meanings. Listen to how the body responds. Tend to the longings of the soul that this word awakens within you. Be open to what it has to say at this moment. Receive the images, feelings, and memories it stirs within you. Let the word speak its meaning and become knit into the fabric of your being. Bring the whole of your life's experience to the reading. Savor all of these experiences and allow them to nourish and bless you; then release them and listen even more deeply to how God is working.

The Gifts of Meditation

Meditation is like a key that unlocks something in our hearts and minds. Another image for meditation is the kaleidoscope that opens up new associations and patterns. The focus of meditation is the heart—a heart receptive to God's presence with us whatever may be happening. It is important to rest with God's Word first, since *being* comes before *doing*. Then we can hear what is emerging inside and allow it to unfold. Before we can figure out what God is saying and respond to it, we must still our minds and open our hearts to listen.

Meditation gives us strength. It is a reservoir of wisdom to deal with life's challenges. It helps us to discern the ways God is calling us out into the world. But first, it invites us on a pilgrimage within, a journey deep into the heart. Meditation allows us to withdraw, to listen deeply, and to be attuned to the Holy Spirit so that we can see our problems in a fresh, new way. It takes us beyond the rationalizations of the mind and leads us into the creative imagination.

Meditatio is the process of allowing the Word to work within us and reflecting on what we have taken into the depths of our being. New insights will come, sometimes while we are meditating, sometimes later in the day as the particular words rise up in our consciousness. Know that this is a part of the process. We can open ourselves and be attentive, but ultimately it is the Spirit who works within us. The Holy Spirit works in its own time and way to bring the inspiration we need. Many layers of insight might need to be revealed to us slowly. We may be taken by surprise to see how God has prepared us for an experience in our life. This is one of the gifts of meditation. Time taken for *lectio divina*, if regular and attentive, will continue to bear fruit in ways we do not expect. This is the work of God within us. If you have ever had a moment when you suddenly understood something in your life in a way that you had not perceived it before, you have experienced grace. The entire book of scripture is a love letter from God. *Lectio divina* keeps this promise alive in us and opens us to new possibilities in the light of this great and tender love. Imagine the many ways God rejoices in us, enjoys our beauty, and nurtures our possibilities. This is the process of a lifetime.

The Poetry of *Lectio Divina*

Reading scripture is like reading poetry. When we read aloud, we can hear the poetry and rhythm of the text. Poetry speaks to parts of us that lie below the threshold of everyday awareness. The rhythm and sound of poetry touches a part of us that ordinary speech cannot reach. Poetry speaks to the imagination and nourishes it.

Imagination is an important element in *lectio divina*. When the imagination responds to the Word, a storehouse of memories is opened up to us. During the Middle Ages, the monks actively used the imagination:

> It permitted them to picture, to "make present," to see beings with all the details provided by the texts: the colors and dimensions of things, the clothing, bearing, and actions of the people, the complex environment in which they move....[B]iblical vocabulary is twofold in character. In the first place, it is often poetic in essence. Sometimes it has greater value because of its power of suggestion than because of its clarity or precision; it hints at much more than it says. But for that very reason it is better suited to express spiritual experience which is completely impregnated with a mysterious light impossible to analyze.[7]

Poetry and metaphor put us in touch with the gifts of our intuitive side and open us up to new possibilities of spiritual experience. As we savor the poetry of scripture, it opens us to new insights and possibilities, new ways of looking at our lives. The words of scripture are rich with metaphors that teach us about who we are and how God might be calling us forward. Actively using the imagination awakens our memories, our hearts, indeed our whole selves to the truths God has for us.

Some Aids to Meditation

There are many things that can enhance your meditation practice. These include committing to a regular time, practicing in a place free from distractions and interruptions, maintaining a good posture, and remembering to breathe fully so that you are grounded in your body. Taking time to memorize some sacred texts is also a helpful way to integrate the Word more fully and deepen your experience of God during meditation. Repeat your word or phrase throughout the day to allow your *lectio divina* time to overflow into your daily life. Something as simple as posting a note in a conspicuous place, or even programming your computer's screensaver to repeat a sacred word, can awaken a sense of God's presence.

Allegorical Sense of Scripture

The second sense of scripture is known as the allegorical or christological sense. This approach focuses on finding deeper, less-obvious layers of Christian meaning in passages of scripture. Reading the scripture through the christological lens involves placing the text within the context of the totality of the Christian story and salvation history. When we read scripture using this lens, the significance of many details and incidents becomes clear to us.

The Hosea passage we have been working with takes place in the desert. This evokes Christ's own visit to the desert (Mark 1:12–13). He was called to this journey as part of his preparation for ministry. In the desert, he faced difficult temptations; it was there that he was also able to gather energy and strength to deal with the things that happened during his time of public ministry. The allegorical sense shows us the value of the desert experience. It teaches us about that place of silence and vulnerability where God can often be heard more clearly. We are invited to follow Christ's example of strength in the face of temptation, of solitude and stillness, and then of service. In Mark's passage we see that listening in the desert comes before action in the world.

Summary

Through meditation we learn how to be with God's Word more deeply. When we take time the text can slowly work its way into the heart. Meditation opens up God's Word for us because we are creating a space for it to interact with our thoughts, feelings, and memories. In this process of unfolding we are allowing God to speak to us where we are. Meditation prepares us to move into the third step of *lectio divina,* where we respond to the movement of God in us.

Practical Applications

- Stop reading and begin to meditate when your heart is touched.
- Create a space for the word or phrase. Reflect on it... Repeat it...memorize it.
- Chew the words slowly and savor them.
- Slow down, taste, linger, and enjoy the words.
- Repeat the words often in your mind and with your voice.
- Allow the words to stir images, feelings, and memories.
- Be open to the way God's Word is working in your heart.
- Notice what is emerging.
- Allow the senses to evoke images and reveal new meanings.
- Listen to how your body responds.

- Tend to the longings awakened by the Word within.
- Allow the Word of God to awaken your imagination.
- Repeat the word or phrase throughout the day; allow *lectio divina* to overflow into daily life.

Example of *Lectio Divina* as Meditation *by Reverend Rosalind Ziccardi*

"I will take you for my wife in righteousness and in justice, in steadfast love, and in mercy. I will take you for my wife in faithfulness; and you shall know the Lord." (Hos 2:19b–20)

I was struck with the idea that God sought marriage—that profoundly and uniquely exclusive union—not friendship, not a business enterprise, not a special connection created with a team or a squad, but marriage, which for God is permanent and not subject to the vagaries of how I feel or how I act. God makes the commitment to me (to *us*, this "Israel" expanded to all who believe in Christ, to all who call on God for our salvation) that I will be neither left behind nor let go. Rooted in God's character, the marriage is permanent, forever, sealed, secure—my place of importance to God is never at risk: *"I will take you for my wife in faithfulness"* (v. 20).

I was drawn back to this repeatedly, and the impact of its implications grew deeper and more affirming. I can run, but I won't be left; I can resist, but I'll never be let go; I can stumble or misunderstand or be diverted from a path of truth as I struggle to interpret God in my life, but my shortcomings, failures, even deliberate rejection won't change God's commitment to me. *But the declaration, the reminder, the statement "You shall know the* LORD*"* was comforting too. Though I often act as if I have the prerogative to "invent" God as I wish God to be, I won't be left to wallow in my vague misunderstandings. I found myself settled by this scripture: God is both knowable and wants to be known. As I come to know my earthly husband, through shared experience and with deliberate purpose, for who he really is—and not who I have presumed him to be—so, too, I am invited to know that God wants to be known and will be revealed for *who God really is.*

It was dawning on me again that God is actively present in my life, in my experience, in my consciousness and my unconscious— where I am aware of trusting and where I don't even know I'm not yet trusting. God's commitment to me isn't governed by my assent or denial, my understanding or ignorance, my trustworthiness, and more to the point, my lack of trustworthiness to this divine commitment. God is God, God is unknowable, and God won't let me go in my capriciousness. God seeks tenderness, personal closeness, and it occurred to me that God wants that closeness like a spouse: for *Godself*—as God engages me for *myself.* Marriage with God isn't designed around "making my life easier" or to "ease my way" or for some other reason connected to having a better life in my human, mortal experience. Nor do I simply serve God to fulfill God's grander purpose. This marriage—this deliberate, tender, loving union—is the grander purpose. That my human experience is richer for knowing this union is undeniable; that I will serve God as I am drawn ever closer into this relationship is probably inevitable. But either way, these are consequences born of a greater reality.

Sitting in my chair in my living room, with my eyes closed and the world quiet, the feeling of warmth and peace was a conscious, if indefinable, sensation. I was relaxed, still, and centered where I instinctively knew it mattered most. I was aware of the next breath I took. I reentered my living room, "my space," and realized that I'd been harboring a fear of "not getting it right" and needing to be reassured that my seeking and desire are useful. But "getting it right" isn't the goal. Reentering self-awareness, I was reassured that God knows about a situation I'm worried about, one that feels "impossible," and that whatever the outcome, God "has me"—won't leave me, or let me go. In this sense of complete security, I feel that I can trust God with the needs of the others in my life, too—for the promise isn't just for me, it extends to include me. I was quiet for several minutes, soaking in the promise of this text.

With another deep breath, I opened my eyes to my familiar surroundings. I looked again at the Bible in my lap and quietly read the whole passage again: "I will take you for my wife in faithfulness." The words are soothing, encouraging, and stimulating. They are hopeful. I smiled as I considered what a staggering promise this is, and I asked God to help me hold that centering truth as I rejoined the activity of my day. How long was I "set apart" in *lectio*? Only about forty minutes, but it felt like I was simply not within earthly time: *chronos* gave way to *kairos*. In those forty earthly minutes I was reminded that eternity with God never stops, and I'm invited in whenever I choose to open the door.

CHAPTER FIVE

Responding to a Touched Heart

Prayer is tasting life. Prayer is responding to life.
—Macrina Wiederkehr, *A Tree Full of Angels*[1]

In the previous chapter we discussed meditation as a way of savoring God's Word. It takes practice to slow down enough to really be present to the Word and to allow it to move within us. When we savor scripture, our hearts are touched and then our response flows.

A Heart That Is Touched

The third step of *lectio divina*, sometimes called *oratio*, meaning "prayer," is the response sparked in us when our hearts have first been touched by God. *Lectio divina* means reading the text, holding the word that beckons us, and allowing it to unfold in our imagination. Prayer begins the moment something stirs in us and touches our heart.

As we have seen, the image of the heart was of primary importance to the ancient biblical writers. The heart is the chief organ of human life located in the very center of our bodies. The heart works hard to pump blood through our system so that we are nourished and energized. In scripture, the heart is a metaphor for the sphere of divine influence; it is the center of our emotional, spiritual, and moral lives.

When we linger with scripture and allow it to permeate our whole being, it nourishes us in ways we can not anticipate. When we savor the Word we begin to really taste life, and out of that experience it is natural for us to respond. This is where prayer rises up within us. Prayer is a response to tasting the reality of things. We begin to see what really *is*, rather than what we *expect* to see.

We each come to scripture with our own set of lenses conditioned by our culture, ethnicity, gender, and economic status. *Lectio divina* challenges us to meet the text on its own terms and move beyond our biases and expectations. We can never fully rid ourselves of our agendas, but we can set them aside as much as possible. Lingering with the Word and allowing it to surprise us lifts us out of our ordinary way of perceiving the world. We begin to see the things around us and within us as God does. William Shannon describes his experience of prayer as "a kind of corrective lens that does away with the distorted view of reality which, for some mysterious reason, seems to be my normal vision and enables me to see what is as it really is."[2] Prayer is our response to the clearer vision that is given to us by God.

When the heart is touched with new vision, there is often a spontaneous response evoked in us. We cannot help but respond when God touches the center of our being, the most intimate and deepest part of us. *Lectio divina* inspires a continuous conversion of the heart. Conversion is the process of falling more deeply in love with God and the world. It means allowing ourselves to be continually surprised by God. Conversion is about allowing our vision to be changed by a God who is much larger than we can imagine.

It would be a mistake to assume that prayer only takes place in the third phase of *lectio. All* of *lectio divina* is a process of moving to deeper and deeper levels of prayer. We need to approach *lectio divina* as a time of prayer from its beginning to its end. We need to let it overflow into our day so that it can continue to unfold and our lives can become prayer. The first two steps of *lectio* are essentially entry points that guide us to deeper prayer. Cistercian monk and scholar Michael Casey writes that for him, *lectio divina* succeeds "only if it causes me to drop my defenses and allow God to touch my heart and change my life."[3] We enter into the fullness of prayer when our hearts of stone begin to soften. Then, holiness flows from an everlasting spring within us and we are moved.

Prayer is not simply a matter of practicing good technique, or gathering knowledge of scripture, or following steps in just the right order. We can never enter into the fullness of prayer if we approach meditation as an intellectual enterprise. Sister Thelma Hall writes, "The goal of prayer is not thoughts or concepts or knowledge *about* God, however sublime, but God himself as he *is,* mysteriously hidden in my deepest, true self." Hall goes on to quote St. Catherine of Siena: "God is my *me*."[4] Prayer is about an encounter with the sacred dimension of reality. It is an experience of knowing God and knowing ourselves more deeply. When we allow ourselves to savor scripture, to take it within ourselves, and to knit it into our very being, what rises up within us spontaneously and naturally is the fullness of prayer.

Saying Yes to God

To understand the distinction between the praying of *lectio divina* as a whole, and the third step, *oratio,* it is necessary to experience the point where we begin to say a full yes to God's work within us.

When your heart is touched, you may notice an invitation rising up within you. This is a sign that something is already flowing in you. Nurture this moment of *lectio* by holding all that has come before and attending to the ways your heart has been moved. Then ask yourself, "What is God's invitation today?" Or, "What is God asking me to look at in my life circumstances right now?" Listen for God's quiet answer and then ask, "How do I say a full *yes* to this invitation?"

Prayer is a living reality. Take time to be with this experience by staying with the words that you have meditated on and then responding from the deepest part of you. There are many ways you can respond to the movement of God within. There's a whole spectrum of emotions that you may be led to express: from grief to gratitude, tenderness to anger. You may want to sing, dance, or laugh. You may need to weep or scream. What comes to us during prayer is not always "sweetness and light." You may become deeply aware of your sorrow or of an unnamed grief you carry over lost opportunities and relationships. A painful memory might be touched and you may need to weep freely. You may feel anger about circumstances in your life or frustrated about being trapped in a situation beyond your control. In your prayer, you may feel God's touch and want to rise up in anger at God. Give yourself permission to feel angry at God over the pain you are experiencing if that's what comes up. Be honest if God feels absent or distant. Say yes to whatever begins to flow inside.

Tears of joy and laughter are given to us as gifts; all emotions show us we are alive; they show us what is important and meaningful. Paying attention to our emotions and giving them room to be expressed are ways to honor the gift of our experience. We see the many ways God can be present to us in both celebration and suffering. The psalms of lament are filled with examples of people expressing their anger through prayer. To deny this painful part of us is to deny our humanity. *Oratio* is an opportunity to recognize what is flowing within our hearts. Saying yes to all that we feel is a continuous prayer of trust in a God who is working within us.

Maria Lichtmann writes that prayer is about receiving the true self that gets hidden by the masks of our daily life. She says that prayer is about receiving the great mystery of reality:

> Prayer includes all three aspects of spiritual practice in their most refined form: prayer brings us to our own *depths,* where "the Spirit intercedes for us with sighs too deep for words" (Rom 8:26); it *relates* us to the world from a place outside our egos; and finally, prayer opens our hearts to the *transcendent Other* in our midst.[5]

Prayer connects us to our deepest self, to the world around us, and to the One who transcends all. When we accept all that we are, we receive all that God has for us within, around, and above.

Prayer as Mutual Striving

Prayer is mutual striving—we awaken to our longing for God and God's longing for us. Savoring the Word is an act of reaching out to meet God. In that encounter we discover the One who is reaching toward us with the same yearning. This is the moment when the heart is touched with the recognition of mutual longing; we realize that God is reaching out to us passionately in response to our hunger: "I strain toward God; God strains toward me. I ache for God; God aches for me. Prayer is mutual yearning, mutual straining, mutual aching."[6] During those moments of prayer, the veil is lifted from our eyes and we begin to discover that there is no real separation between ourselves and God.

Prayer is what opens us up to receiving the love of God, the ever-present, radiant love that is reaching out to us. We can either receive or reject this love. Prayer helps us to soften our hearts and respond to our longing for God. Thelma Hall describes how God works in and through our longing:

> It is this intrinsic longing which is awakened in prayer when we allow ourselves to be vulnerable and, putting aside our defenses and masks, stand before God in our naked need and creaturehood. The time comes when we realize that this longing is itself the presence of God's longing in us. Meanwhile, *Oratio* is the active effort we make to keep our hearts open to him and to put ourselves at the disposal of his Spirit, preparing the way for God's action to supersede our own.[7]

Our longing keeps us related to the sacred. When we pray a prayer of vulnerability and tenderness, we can receive the fullness of God.

Holy Desire

One of the fruits of the prayer experience is an increase in our desire for God. When we allow our hearts to respond spontaneously to God's movement toward us, we will recognize that God is as close to us as our breath. Some barriers we experience are created by us. Growing in holy desire means that "God creates in us a greater capacity for himself, not only by our longing but sometimes through the very frustration and powerlessness we experience as we reach out blindly toward him."[8] Our absolute vulnerability draws us like a magnetic force toward the One who is our center of gravity, and the experience of separateness from God gives way to unity with God. This center is also the dwelling place of our true selves. The more we surrender to this force and give up our illusions of separation, the more we experience the sense of God dwelling within us. Desire for God draws us to prayer and prayer shows us God's presence everywhere.

Holy Rhythm of *Lectio Divina*

As we have already mentioned, *lectio divina* is *not* a set of techniques to be mastered or tools to be acquired. The steps we are outlining are only a helpful *framework* for the journey. Each stage of *lectio* has its own features and questions. However, the most essential part to remember is that the steps are meant to be a living rhythm of surrendering to God and receiving from God. We surrender our barriers to intimacy with God; we receive God's unfolding grace and love.

Learning the rhythm of *lectio* could be compared to learning to play an instrument—for example, the cello. We first learn how to handle the instrument. The bow is resined and placed on the strings in varying positions and with different pressures. Finding the notes on each of the strings requires knowing the position and placement. Creating a vibrato also involves a certain kind of movement with our fingers. As our skill develops, we do not need to be as attentive to our physical manipulations. Eventually the instrument becomes second nature and we can play with ease. The *cellist* becomes an instrument through which the music seems almost to play itself. With *lectio*, using the ladder approach is much like learning how to handle the instrument. When we are at ease with *lectio*, the Spirit and we are one and we move however we are invited to by God.[9]

The heart of *lectio divina* is a gradual process of moving more and more deeply into our desires and God's desires for us until we recognize that our deepest desires have been placed there by God. Esther de Waal describes this experience as "a heartbeat inside of [our] own self....It is as though we now allow ourselves to be drawn to him as though with a magnet, and all the false self, with its games and facades, falls away and instead we surrender totally to God."[10] The image of a heartbeat captures the sense of God's pulse beating within us, always inviting us to a deeper relationship. *Lectio divina* opens us to a holy rhythm of life where our whole being is drawn down through deeper and deeper layers. While we can do much to make ourselves available to an awareness of God's presence, ultimately this is not our work at all. We can only make space for our hearts to be touched by the love of God. *Lectio divina* is about creating space for God to work and about freeing ourselves from the distractions and burdens of our lives. Then the movement and rhythm of desire for God and surrender to God can unfold naturally and spontaneously.

The rhythm of God's loving presence extends beyond any formal *time* of prayer. God wants the holy rhythm of *lectio divina* to shape our lives. Sometimes our hearts are touched later in the day when our formal *lectio* prayer is over. We may see a word or phrase from our earlier prayer time in a new light. When an insight or word comes to us during the day, we are allowing God's presence to spill over into the whole of our lives and are opening ourselves to the gift of a touched heart at any time. God wants to be able to touch our hearts at any moment of the day.

The Practice of *Lectio Divina*:
The Third Step—Praying with God's Word

The previous chapter addressed the second movement of *lectio*, meditation. We learned how to savor the Word and allow it to unfold in the imagination where it evokes images, feelings, and memories. In this chapter, we have been discussing the third step of *lectio divina—oratio.*

After you have taken time to meditate on the text, read the scripture passage again and allow yourself to be present to the ways you have been touched by the words. Consider what implications they have for your life today. God speaks to each of us right where we are, in the midst of the concrete circumstances of our lives. Allow yourself to be touched and to receive the invitation to something new. Notice how your heart responds to this invitation.

The heart prays in many different ways. Sometimes your prayer will be simple gratitude or you may feel awe and joy. Sometimes your prayer will lead to grief and you will need to weep freely. You may or may not know the root of this sorrow. However, the important thing is to give it space and know that it is being released. Sometimes your prayer will come out of a place of anger at some injustice and you need to cry out. Other times the invitation is just to notice life more deeply, to spend more time in silence. Sometimes you will be challenged to look at the life-giving (and life-draining) activities that take up your time. Remember to trust that whatever rises up in you is your prayer response. Allow yourself to be present to any genuine, heartfelt prayer. Too often we push away uncomfortable feelings or we long only for joy in prayer. But we are called to be true to God and to our feelings. This is the holy rhythm of an authentic relationship with self and God.

There are times of prayer when we do not feel touched at all, when we are at a loss for words or feelings. Everyone experiences these times of spiritual dryness. Michael Casey's suggestions might be helpful at such times:

> [I]f prayer is not found then insert it. Begin the reading with a prayer, interrupt the text with prayer. Some people find it useful to translate each verse that they read into an address to God that springs from the reality of their own

life and experience. Most often, if we tackle a text in this way and demonstrate our seriousness, the impermeable façade will crack and spontaneous prayer will begin to tumble from the text. This is because the apparent prayer-lessness of a text is more often really a matter of our sub-jective dispositions. When we get in touch with our desire to pray and leave aside the obtrusive inner resistances that block our endeavor, things go better.[11]

One way to get in touch with feelings is to simply rest with the question of what you feel the invitation might be at the time. It might help to ask yourself: "What does God want me to hear right now?" Or, "What are some ways for me to hear more clearly?" It is important to turn your attention to the needs of the ones you love, the needs of your community, and the needs of the world. You might simply want to rest in a sense of your own love radiating out into the world.

Moral Sense of Scripture

The moral, or behavioral, sense of scripture refers to the way God's Word shapes our beliefs and values so that we slowly live into the meaning of them. It does not refer to the ethical content of scripture. When scripture leads us to live out our prayer through action in our day we are embodying the moral sense.

The Scriptures are given to form our behavior, to make us Christlike. Whatever they impart by way of informa-tion—including theological information—is secondary to their role in the practical reformation of daily life accord-ing to the teaching and example of Jesus. "Blessed are those who hear God's word—and keep it" (Luke 11:28). As Saint James reminds us, we are called to be "doers of the word and not hearers only" (James 1:22–25).[12]

In the Hosea passage we see how the moral, or behavioral, sense can speak to us. Time spent in the wilderness with God opens us up to a more intimate relationship with God: "Therefore, I will now persuade her, and bring her into the wilderness, and speak tenderly to her" (Hos 2:14). When we experience love in a relationship, it affects our behavior. Love helps us live life out of a more grateful and faithful stance. Love gives us energy. This energy grows as we relate to others. We see ourselves and others in a more life-giving way. The spark ignited by our experience of God's love flows into our behavior; we want to love others as God has loved us. The tenderness and mercy we have experienced with God enables us to be more compassionate with ourselves and others. Our response to others comes from being well loved by God. We behave and live with a greater sense of righteousness and justice. Our world enlarges. Love takes us out of ourselves. We begin to realize that our local world is a global world: right relationships exist between individuals but they also extend to right relationships with all peoples.

The wilderness motif in Hosea reminds us of the value of reflection when we are in the wilderness. Through reflection in the wilderness, we can be gifted with insight about what it means to experience our beliefs and to live out of those beliefs. If we believe we are in a covenant relationship with God, how does that affect the way we behave with others? If we believe in God's steadfast love and faithfulness, how does that affect the way we live with challenge and conflict? If we believe in mercy, how does that affect the compassion we extend to others? God is at the heart of how we live our beliefs and values. Our relationship with God shapes who we are and how we behave. Prayer without action or service to others is really not prayer.

Summary

Prayer is a natural response to that moment when God touches the heart. Prayer means listening for God's Word to us and then saying yes. Prayer may stir up a wide range of feelings but we can learn to honor them by giving them space. During a time of prayer we tap into our desire for God and discover God is constantly moving toward us. There are many ways that we can strive to express our longing for God. Although prayer is ultimately expressed in service, it is not always about *doing* something; it is about being in relationship with someone. Sometimes all we need to "do" is to rest in the presence of God. Gradually, God's love will draw us into *contemplatio*. Contemplation is the wordless prayer of simply being aware of God's loving presence.

Practical Applications

- Respond when your heart is first touched. That spark is prayer.
- Remember that *all* aspects of *lectio* can be prayer.
- Stay with the words you have meditated on and then respond from the deepest part of you. Pay attention to the emotions evoked.
- Savor the Word and respond out of that experience.
- Discover the mutual longing between you and God.
- Ask yourself, "What is God's invitation to me today?"
- Respond in prayer.
- Be open to saying yes to God's work within you.
- Let *lectio* overflow into your day so that your life becomes a prayer.

Example of *Lectio Divina* as Prayer by *Reverend Rosalind Ziccardi*

I will take you for my wife in righteousness and in justice, in steadfast love, and in mercy. I will take you for my wife in faithfulness; and you shall know the LORD. (Hos 2:19b–20).

I love you, God.

How can I possibly love *you*? An audacious statement, it seems: *you* who are Almighty, Maker of heaven and earth, *you* in whom even the *idea* of loving is born. My love for *you* is *your* love in some foundational way and yet it is *my* love expression, unique to me, *my* singular self that is *not* my son or husband or neighbor. And even if "my" love is born in *your* heart, it is returned through my heart—this small, puny, speck-of-sand-on-the-beaches-of-the-world heart that *you* created, know, and inspire with love. *This* heart feels *that* love and realizes, in a small way, that it loves *you* however it can, in however limited a way, however selfishly expressed. (For I need you completely. My life *isn't* without you.) And this heart overflows, bursts its banks like a swollen river floods over, to realize that *you* love me. In some way, like a baby's glad spark of recognition that thrills the mother who bore it, my spark of love pleases *you*. How incomplete I am not to know it to be true. Thank *you* (again) for your initiating love. Thank *you* (again) for the privilege to love *you* and to know that I do.

CHAPTER SIX

Contemplative Awakening and Awareness

Awareness of God, at its deepest level, is not so much
something we *do* as something we *are*.
—William Shannon, *Silence on Fire*[1]

The previous step of *oratio*, the response of the heart that has
been touched, eventually leads us into *contemplatio*, the wordless
prayer of contemplation. During contemplative prayer we experience the presence of God permeating our being.

What Is Contemplation?

Theologian Walter Burghardt draws on the words of William
McNamara to describe contemplation as "a long, loving look at
the real."[2] Contemplation can be considered long because it takes
time to enter a contemplative space. Contemplation requires love
rooted in One who is the ground of love and the ground of our
being. What is real is the very substance of our lives. The real is
not always beautiful or wonderful—often it is painful and difficult. To look unhurriedly, with love, at what is most deeply real
and to cultivate this posture in the whole of our lives is to cultivate a contemplative way of being.

Thomas Merton (1915–68), a Trappist monk and poet,
described contemplation as the highest expression of a person's
spiritual life: "It is that life itself, fully awake, fully active, fully
aware that it is alive. It is spiritual wonder. It is spontaneous awe

at the sacredness of life, of being."³ Contemplation is a profound realization that life proceeds from an invisible, transcendent, and infinitely abundant Source. Contemplation means cultivating a way of being fully present to God in a loving and unhurried way. With time and practice, we will bring this awareness of God's presence to every moment of our lives. We will eventually find ourselves following Paul's invitation to "pray without ceasing" (1 Thess 5:17).

The previous steps of *lectio* are all active: we read, we listen, and we respond. When we enter contemplative prayer we are still; we are before God. We are invited to simply *be* with the insights we have received in our prayer and to *be* with God. The aim of contemplation is for God to be our all, our very life-breath. Contemplation is first and foremost a *gift*. We can create space for contemplation in our lives but ultimately the ability to move into a loving state of being and stillness is a gift from the One who is the Source of All Love. Contemplation is sometimes described as wordless prayer because we return to the very Source of prayer and to the Word who is beyond all words and names.

Kataphatic and Apophatic Prayer

The Christian tradition has identified two primary paths of prayer. The first form corresponds to *oratio*. *Kataphatic* prayer is known as the "path of images." As Christians, we believe that God is revealed through creation. Matter can be a window that gives us a glimpse of God. We use metaphors and images drawn from the material world because it's the only way we can speak of the One who is above and beyond this world. The kataphatic way is the great path of artists and poets who reveal the sacred through icons and music, poetry and dance. Images are a way to explore the sacred; they reveal to us the mysterious nature of God's sacred presence.

The second form of prayer corresponds to *contemplatio*. *Apophatic* prayer is known as the "path of unknowing." Images help us express our experience of God and move us closer to the divine but they only *point* to the sacred. Words and images limit us. Ultimately, they fail to reveal the fullness of who God is. All the great religious traditions of the world, and all the marvelous collection of ways we have to celebrate God, cannot fully express the depth and fullness of the divine. The first three stages of *lectio divina* are a process of knowing about God. With contemplation we move into a process of *unknowing*. We let go of our dependence on thoughts, words, and images. Contemplative prayer is apophatic prayer. After we have listened to the images and feelings that scripture evokes in us, we recognize that God is not contained in any of them. We honor God as one who is greater than anything we can imagine.

Apophatic prayer is not any "better" than kataphatic prayer. They are essentially two complementary movements in our longing for God that must be held together in gentle tension. When we hold too tightly to any particular image of God, we risk idolatry. Contemplation helps us loosen our grip on any particular image or idea and frees us to simply experience God.

Awareness

Contemplation is fundamentally an awareness of the presence of God in our lives. Everything in life is sacred. Contemplative awareness opens our hearts to see something of God that we would not see otherwise. We learn to see God in each person, event, and situation. Thomas Merton describes contemplation as a gift of awareness that is the goal of life:

> [It is] an awakening to the real that is within all that is real. A vivid awareness of infinite Being at the roots of our own limited being....Contemplation is also the response to a call: a call from Him Who has no voice, and yet Who speaks in everything that is, and Who, most of all, speaks in the depths of our own being: for we ourselves are words of His.[4]

Lectio divina begins with the Word of God and leads us slowly toward an increasing awareness of the way God dwells within us and invites us to become God's words in the world. The process essentially means disposing ourselves to be aware of the presence of God in all things. Contemplative awareness is a qualitatively different experience than thinking. The thinking brain analyzes, compartmentalizes, and evaluates. To do that it needs to separate itself from the thing it is studying. Contemplative prayer is unitive; it closes the gap between us and God: "A *true sense* of awareness...*closes the gap* between me and that of which I am aware. It brings us together. It unites."[5]

Prayer of Union

In our previous chapter we discussed the mutual striving that occurs between ourselves and God. Yearning for God means we let the life that is flowing within us connect us to life everywhere, in every one, at all times and for all time. Contemplation draws us out of ourselves and more deeply into ourselves at the same time. Contemplation teaches us to give the self over to oneness with the God who is already there, who is closer to us than we are to ourselves. We come to recognize that God dwells so intimately within us that nothing can separate us from God. William Shannon tells this story:

> One day a lover approached the home of his Beloved. He knocked on the door. A Voice within responded to the knocking: "Who is there?" The Lover answered: "It is I." The Voice within spoke, almost sadly: "There is no room here for me and thee."
>
> The Lover went away and spent much time trying to learn the meaning of the words of his Beloved. Then one day, some time later, he once again approached the home of his Beloved and, as before, he knocked on the door. Once again, as had happened earlier, the Voice within asked: "Who is there?" This time the Lover answered: "It

is Thou." And the door opened and he entered the home of his Beloved.[6]

Slowly, little by little, we see the barriers we put up between ourselves and God. The answer *"It is Thou"* comes as we gradually see only God in us. Prayer is really nothing more than coming into greater consciousness of what already dwells within us and within every person and creature.

In contemplative prayer we pray until wordlessness takes over. God's presence becomes more palpable than words. We move beyond ideas of God into an experience of God. We allow the heart of God to pulse in our own hearts. Often our prayers can be too focused on a particular goal. Contemplation invites us to let go of our goals and simply rest in the meaning of all of life, which is love. The fruit of contemplative prayer is inner peace, quiet, and joy.

Kairos Time and *Chronos* Time

The Greeks have two words for time: *chronos* time, which is linear and orderly, and *kairos* time, which is qualitative. *Chronos* time depends on day-planners and clocks. It is the dominant way we move through our lives in this culture. We rush from one event to another and measure our worth by how productive we have been. We check off tasks on our "to-do list" and wake up each morning to a whole new list waiting for us. When *chronos* rules, we live in a world of scarcity, and nothing is ever finished.

Kairos time is God's time: time for stillness and beauty, time for being, Sabbath time. While *chronos* time is quantitative, *kairos* time is qualitative. We are so immersed in the moment that we lose track of time; we step outside of the here and now and touch the eternal. It is the moment when something opens up. We are lifted from our everyday concerns and become fully present to the moment. In *kairos* time we become completely engaged by the moment and immersed in a sense of flow. We are so enthralled by the journey that we forget to worry about end results. When we cultivate a contemplative spirit, God can break through in "the right time" and surprise us with grace. A contemplative spirit makes loving, praying, creating, birthing, and dying an experience of holiness.

In our culture, we often allow *chronos* time to seize us and take over. We can never put work aside. We become slaves to our doing. With every project we say yes to, we may be saying no to the holy pauses, those moments when God wants to speak. We live in a world that places a high value on speed and productivity, and the pace of life keeps increasing despite technological advances designed to save us time. Contemplation slows us down so that we can experience being not just doing. The pressure to work harder and harder can draw us away from time for personal renewal and prayer. It moves us further from what is most valuable in life. We need to reject the superficialities of life and carve out time for contemplation so that we can reclaim what is most real: the experience of God.

The spiritual life does not operate in high gear at full speed. The faster we go, the more we leave ourselves behind. Time is a gift given for the sake of discovery. There is a great deal to be discovered in life before we are finally able to break open to the God within and around us. Time is the gift of realization that wherever we are, whatever is happening, is the stuff of God. A contemplative will begin to live more of his or her life in *kairos* time, where each moment is a sacrament revealing God to us in the here and now.

The Role of Silence

Earlier in the book we discussed the importance of cultivating an attitude of deep listening to the world and the essential role silence plays in moving us into an awareness of God's loving presence. Contemplative prayer deepens our experience of God through silence.

The clatter of our lives only serves to protect us from really listening to ourselves and God. Silence brings us face to face with ourselves; it is the void in the center of the soul where we meet God. Active interior silence will bring us deep into the heart of God where we are whole. As we spend time in contemplative prayer, the quality of our silence changes. We experience a greater receptivity. Stillness quiets and calms our being. We can see what is happening deep inside us. Silence creates space and teaches us to taste and smell life in a new way. We experience God in a new way. The great mystic Meister Eckhart said: "Nothing is so like God as silence."[7]

True Self and False Self

We arrive in this world created in the image of God, each with unique gifts to offer. Thomas Merton described this gifted self as the *true self*—the self planted in us by God. The *false self* is the part of us that blocks the true self and prevents us from hearing its voice. The true self wants nothing more or less than for us to be the whole, beautiful person God created us to be. The true core of our being is like a wave in the ocean of God, a flame in God's fire. Merton said there is a hidden wholeness in all things. This hidden wholeness is who we truly are. Through contemplation, God can release us from the tyranny of a false self so that our true nature can thrive. It moves us toward a greater awareness of our wholeness in God.[8] Merton describes his own experience of complete surrender to God in his book *New Seeds of Contemplation:* "I break through the superficial exterior appearances that form my routine vision of the world and of my own self, and I find myself in the presence of hidden majesty."[9] Merton describes the hidden majesty of the true inner self as a jewel brought up from the bottom of the sea.[10]

Most of us live our lives predominantly under the influence of the false self. The false self is the ego self that distorts our self-image by either inflating or deflating us. It is the intellectual self that wants to hover above the mess of life in the world of ideas. It is the ethical self that wants to live by some abstract moral code rather than wrestle with the realities of life. The false self is the part of us that holds on too tightly to anything other than God or that puts God in a comfortable box. It includes the masks we wear and the things we do for the approval of others. We can lose ourselves when we surrender to the expectations of our family or a demanding job. We lose our balance when we are distracted by busyness or possessions. When we place more importance on people or things than they merit, we are operating out of our false selves. The illusions we live under, the anxieties and fears that haunt us, are all parts of the superficial world of the false self.

The Spanish mystic and doctor of the church Teresa of Avila, in her book *The Interior Castle,* describes the soul as a jewel, a diamond castle filled with many rooms. The center room is the place of the most intimate communion with God. Attachments and false masks keep us from entering this holy and hidden room deep within. Teresa writes that when we reach that final room of the soul, the scales are removed from our eyes and we finally see how truly beautiful we are.[11] Uncovering the true self is a lifelong process of recognizing that we are unique reflections of God; we are revelations of God in this world. As we surrender our false selves to God through contemplation, our hearts become aligned with God's desires and the true self in all its beauty is revealed to us.

New Vision

The practice of contemplation awakens us to a new vision and shapes our vision of reality. We see everything, including ourselves, with greater consciousness and love. Vision is a quality of the soul. A contemplative spirit sees God everywhere, and all of creation becomes illuminated by the sacred. Contemplation connects us to the divine source of love, the ground of our being. We see God in our deepest hungers and longings. Contemplative prayer is a practice that "reminds us that we are not flat surfaces but mysterious depths which cannot be plumbed directly through what we think and what we do."[12] Contemplation joins us to the One who dwells within, and enables us to see the world with God's eyes.

Contemplation is an expression of the divine-human partnership that gives us eyes to see things *as they are* and with love. This loving gaze, however, requires a sense of openness; it involves risk. We might need to ask ourselves whether we are looking at things as they truly are or as we would like to them to be. Do we want to confirm what we already think or discover something new? Will we allow God to challenge us to live out a new vision of reality? Are we open to being surprised by the grace of God as it is revealed in others?

Contemplation enables us to see things from a spacious perspective that is rooted in time and reality. It involves developing our own compassionate attention. When we begin to see the truth below the surface of things we are more able to listen to the voices that go unheard. German theologian Dorothee Soelle says: "The soul that is united with God sees the world with God's eyes. That soul, like God, sees what otherwise is rendered invisible and irrelevant."[13] Gazing at reality does not always involve beauty and wonder, but the practice of contemplative living increases our capacity for bearing the truth and becoming more authentically human.

Contemplative prayer-practices are often "marketed" as an antidote to the toxicity of modern life, to anyone who feels overwhelmed or alienated by their work. A true contemplative spirituality seeks to enter more fully into the depths of reality by resting in God's presence while God works in the soul. Contemplation can help us slow down for a moment and cope better with the stresses of life, but this is a benefit, not the main purpose of contemplation.

Contemplation, Communion, and Community

Contemplation is a gift of awareness that helps us to break through the superficialities of life and see the world in a new way.

Contemplative living leads to a transformation of the self. This transformation is an awakening to the sacredness of everything and everyone, especially those who dwell on the margins, those who are so often unseen. From a long, loving look at the world comes communion, "the discovery of the Holy in deep, thoughtful encounters—with God's creation, with God's people, with God's self—where love is proven by sacrifice, the wild exchange of all for another, for the Other."[14] Prayer with God opens us up to communion with all of creation.

Merton describes the ultimate perfection of the contemplative life as "not a heaven of separate individuals, each one viewing his [or her] own private intuition of God; it is a sea of Love which flows through the One Body of all the elect."[15] Contemplation may initially lead us more deeply into solitude and silence, but true contemplative experiences always lead us back to a more profound awareness of how deeply we are connected to all of creation. We are initiated into a new relationship with God, ourselves, other people, and the cosmos. The experience of contemplation leads us to loving awareness of our sisters and brothers. Relationships become deeper and fuller. We laugh more and cry more as we open ourselves to more of creation. We are able to lovingly embrace all that arises and give the increased pain and tears back to God. "The contemplative finds the Ground of Love in all reality."[16] This leads to a deep sense of connectedness and communion. We can never separate contemplation from engagement with the needs of the world.

The Practice of *Lectio Divina*: The Fourth Step—Contemplation

Contemplation may flow naturally from our experience of the first steps of *lectio*. We move from reading the Word, to savoring individual words and allowing them to unfold within us. God touches our hearts and we respond with a yes to an invitation toward transformation. This leads to *contemplatio*, which is a prayer of soaking, of simply basking in the experience of love, of allowing that love to work its transforming renewal within. *Contemplatio* may also occur spontaneously.

After we have given ourselves time to dwell with the prayer that rises up in us, we move ourselves gently into contemplative prayer. Begin by simply resting in the silence and the sense of God's presence you have already received. Let go and breathe in this awareness that God is intimately present and entwined in our lives.

Centering Prayer

There are many ways to enter into the contemplative experience. In modern times, the practice of centering prayer has been a great doorway for many people to practice contemplative prayer and rest in God's loving presence. Centering prayer was developed from a practice described in the anonymous fourteenth-century contemplative classic *The Cloud of Unknowing*.[17] "Centering Prayer is a method designed to facilitate the development of contemplative prayer by preparing our faculties to receive this gift....It is at the same time a relationship with God and a discipline to foster that relationship. This method of prayer is a movement beyond conversation with Christ to communion with Him."[18] Centering prayer involves trusting and resting in God, without thought or focus on anything. It is essentially a prayer of companionable silence.

To practice centering prayer, first select a word that is a symbol of your intention to consent to God's presence and action within. Make this selection prayerfully. As the author of *The Cloud of Unknowing* suggests, "[a] one-syllable word such as 'God' or 'Love' is best."[19] Then, sitting comfortably and with your eyes closed, allow yourself to be in silence, resting in God. Whenever you notice your mind engaged with thoughts, gently introduce the sacred word to help you disengage from your thoughts. For some persons, instead of a sacred word, noticing one's breath or a simple inward glance toward the Divine Presence may be more suitable. Do not use your sacred word, breath, or sense of Presence as a focus point. Use it as a small tool to help you disengage from—or drop beneath—the inevitable thoughts that fill our minds. Continue the practice for twenty minutes (if you are able). At the end of your practice period, gently draw your attention back to your surroundings. You may wish to end the practice period with a gentle recitation of the Lord's Prayer or a psalm. Ease back into an awareness of the world around you. To fully appreciate the character of centering prayer, it is recommended that we practice it twenty minutes, twice a day, for about three months. It's important to remember that the natural setting of centering prayer is sacred silence. You simply devote time to the practice and trust God to make good use of that time. With regular practice you may begin to notice more peacefulness or clarity in how you react to life's events.[20]

The Mystical Sense of Scripture

The mystical or unitive sense of scripture means that the passage invites us into an experience of union with God through meeting God in the text. Scripture has the power to increase our holy desire for God and lead us more deeply into our prayer.

In classical theology, the contemplative journey is divided into three stages: purgation, illumination, and union. The first stage of purgation is a desert experience of being stripped of all of one's comforts and securities, of all of the false hopes and visions we have for our lives. It is a purging of the ego or the false self. It is emptying ourselves of illusions. This moves us toward greater freedom. We realize that the things we cling to so tightly are not important. Purgation is a place where relationships are deepened because we finally see how precious others are to us. The desert is where God meets us as we embrace our most vulnerable selves and we realize that nothing is certain in this human existence. For most of us, the desert is not a literal place but an experience that takes hold of us and turns us inside out.[21]

The purgative encounter with God leads to the second stage, where we experience illumination. This transformation is always a gift of grace, but it is also a result of letting go of what we no longer need and focusing on what is most important to us. The experience of illumination can often require a long and often-agonizing time of waiting for insight.[22] This leads to the experience of union: we come to know the God who dwells within ourselves and all of creation. We come to the realization that all of our doing means nothing compared to who we are called to be with God. We are called to love deeply and tenderly and openly. Our doing flows from this place of being. We may begin doing less, but doing it more intentionally. But we do so only after we have cleared space within ourselves to simply be with God.[23]

Summary

Contemplation is a prayer of loving awareness where we move beyond the image we have of God into an experience of resting in the silence of God's presence. Through contemplative prayer we grow in union with God and all of creation. We release the attachments of the false self and become more deeply who we were created to be.

Practical Applications

- Release all words, images, or thoughts.
- Be open to God's gift of contemplation by just being in silence.
- Select a one- or two-syllable word or image that is a symbol of your intention to consent to God's presence or action within.
- Sit comfortably with your eyes closed, resting in God.
- Be fully present to God.
- End your prayer practice by gently drawing your attention back to your surroundings.
- End the practice period, if you wish, with a gentle recitation of the Lord's Prayer or a psalm.

CHAPTER SEVEN

Lectio as Scripture Study, Prayer, and Living

> Monastic *lectio* is the practice of reading small passages daily—
> a page, a paragraph, a sentence—and then milking for
> meaning any word or phrase or situation that interests or
> provokes me there. Then the soul wrestling begins.
> —Joan Chittister, *Illuminated Life*[1]

We have looked at how God communicates with us through scripture and all of life. In the previous chapter we learned about the way of contemplation and the gifts it brings us. In this chapter we will explore new possibilities: *lectio divina* as a means of study, a prayer experience, and a way of living.

Some people ground their experience of *lectio* first, by doing a thorough study of the sacred text. This usually involves the literal sense of the text. For others, the study of *lectio divina* is primarily about the prayer experience itself. They approach *lectio* more as a way of life than a way of thinking and learning. All forms of *lectio* bring us into a direct encounter with God's Word and have the potential to lead us to a more intimate relationship with God and life.

Scripture scholar Walter Brueggemann identifies three rhythms of life in his book *The Message of the Psalms:* orientation, disorientation, and new orientation.[2] *Lectio* can help us see how these rhythms operate in our lives so that we can live them with God's grace. Brueggemann applies his three rhythms of life to the psalms. His approach to the psalms can enrich the *lectio* experience and lead us to a more intimate relationship with God and life. In this chapter we will use his rhythms of life with several psalms as a way of studying scripture with *lectio divina*.

Lectio Divina Study as a Way of Becoming

As we learned, *lectio divina* is a way of being with self, God, and all of life. Irene Nowell, in an article entitled "The Psalms: Living Water of Our Lives," adds another dimension to our understanding of *lectio*: "As we pray the psalms daily, what kind of people are we becoming?"[3] We could broaden this question and ask: "As we study and pray scripture using *lectio divina*, what kind of people are we becoming?" We believe scripture is God's way of communicating with us, shaping us, and forming us.

Until the twelfth century, *lectio divina* was a way of study, prayer, and living. Observing and practicing the monastic life were considered essential parts of study. Monastic scholar Jean Leclercq, in *The Love of Learning and the Desire for God*, says:

> The scholastic *lectio* takes the direction of the *quaestio* and the *disputatio*. The reader puts questions to the text and then questions himself on the subject matter: *quaeri solet*. The monastic *lectio* is oriented toward the *meditatio* and the *oratio*. The objective of the first is science and knowledge; of the second, wisdom and appreciation. In the monastery, the *lectio divina*, which begins with grammar, terminates in compunction, in desire of heaven.[4]

Lectio divina, for the monastic, involved the whole person: it began with the head but always ended with the work of the heart.

Our focus now will be on the monastic way of studying scripture. Reading done in a slow, reflective way awakens the soul to appreciate new meanings. Meditation empties the mind of thoughts, it empties the heart of emotions, and it empties the body of displaced energy. Meditation enables us to make space to receive new thoughts and reflections: "*Meditatio*, in its classical use, means a deep study, thinking out a subject....As the monk pronounced the words aloud he could hear new meanings, meanings that he didn't get when he was thinking silently."[5] Prayer then becomes a dialogue about these new meanings as they affect my life and the lives of others in the world. If we are receptive to what is being shaped deep inside, we are invited to communion and oneness with the new insight. When we act on this new wisdom it is the natural response of a grateful heart.

Three Rhythms of Life

Psalms of Orientation

When we experience life as stable, balanced, safe, and orderly, we feel confident and successful. Brueggemann finds this experience of life expressed in what he calls psalms of orientation. These psalms reveal a God who is reliable and trustworthy. When we are in this phase of life we envision a God who is faithful, stable, and good. All of life speaks of the Creator.[6]

Psalm 8

[1] O LORD, our Sovereign,
how majestic is your name in all the earth!

You have set your glory above the heavens.
[2] Out of the mouths of babes and infants
you have founded a bulwark because of your foes,
to silence the enemy and the avenger.

[3] When I look at your heavens, the work of your fingers,
the moon and the stars that you have established;

[4] what are human beings that you are mindful of them,
mortals that you care for them?

[5] Yet you have made them a little lower than God,
and crowned them with glory and honor.

⁶ You have given them dominion over the works of your hands;
  you have put all things under their feet,

⁷ all sheep and oxen,
  and also the beasts of the field,

⁸ the birds of the air, and the fish of the sea,
  whatever passes along the paths of the seas.

⁹ O LORD, our Sovereign,
  how majestic is your name in all the earth!

We invite you to use *lectio divina* to study Psalm 8, a song of orientation. Read the psalm slowly. As you read, try to understand what God wants to show you. Read aloud slowly with an open heart and listen to what word or phrase speaks to you. There are a number of phrases that you can focus on for study and prayer:

- How majestic is your name! (vv. 1b, 9b)
- You have founded a bulwark. (v. 2b)
- What are human beings that you are mindful of them? (v. 4a)
- You have made them a little lower than God. (v. 5a)
- You have given them dominion. (v. 6a)

Spend time savoring a word or phrase that is meaningful and be attentive to the faith God is forming in you.

Different phrases in Psalm 8 will evoke different feelings for each person. The feelings all have the quality of security and hope that is characteristic of the psalms of orientation. Awe may stir you if you choose *How majestic is your name!* Your time spent feeling wonder at God's greatness might lead you to reflect on what a privilege it is to come to know God. Psalm 8 begins *and* ends with *How majestic is your name!* Awe starts with God and leads us back to God, our Source and Goal. If you reflect on *You have founded a bulwark,* you may feel a sense of the security God provides and be led to praise the God of solidity and strength. You might feel joy about the personal attention God gives to each of us if you choose *What are human beings that you are mindful of them?* Another choice might be *You have made them a little lower than God*. This phrase tells us that we are given a privileged position; human beings are made in the image of God and are able to be co-creators with God. Finally, *You have given them dominion* reminds us that God shares authority and power with us. We are given stewardship over ourselves and all of creation.

Our reflections and new understandings lead us to greater awe and wonder. We marvel: Who are *we* that we are invited to praise God? We wonder: Who are *we* that we are made co-creators with God? This experience of awe and wonder leads us to praise God. It might also invite us to just rest in God.

As we read, meditate, and pray with Psalm 8, we are given an overview of how we are oriented toward God and life. In this text we can look at how the psalmist experiences the awe and glory of God. We can marvel at God's name and at how God is personally involved with human beings. The psalmist reveals God as Creator and Artisan. We, too, experience God creating us and crafting us; we see God creating *through* us. We are made only a little less than God, are favored by God, and are given responsibility for creation. With the psalmist, we can praise this great and wonderful God who is always blessing us. We celebrate our humanity and recognize our fragility. We respond to our call to be stewards and reflect on our stewardship of the earth for the sake of justice and righteousness. We find our ultimate destiny is to praise God. We grow in awareness of our blessed state and our actions flow from that knowledge. We become appreciative, grateful people. As we hold this *lectio divina* in our memory, it becomes part of who we are. When we need it, we are reminded about what we have learned and experienced. Our response to life is rooted in our sense of who we are becoming: artisans and co-creators with God. This psalm gives us an opportunity to experience a moment of orientation; it enables us to experience *lectio divina* as a time of gratitude and celebration.

Psalms of Disorientation

Sometimes it is difficult to be aware of our blessings. Walter Brueggemann speaks of this as the phase of disorientation. Disorientation can be caused by external circumstances or internal conditions. We are in this stage when we experience life as chaotic, dark, and painful. We wonder where God is in all this. We feel as though God has abandoned us. Although we have *learned* that God is always with us, this is not what we are *experiencing* in the moment. Darkness obscures that vision. Our dominant focus becomes coping with sadness and pain. All we can do is feel our pain, cry out, and beg God to deliver us.[7]

Psalm 13

[1] How long, O LORD? Will you forget me forever?
How long will you hide your face from me?
[2] How long must I bear pain in my soul,
and have sorrow in my heart all day long?
How long shall my enemy be exalted over me?

[3] Consider and answer me, O LORD my God!
Give light to my eyes, or I will sleep the sleep of death,
[4] and my enemy will say, "I have prevailed";
my foes will rejoice because I am shaken.

[5] But I trusted in your steadfast love;
my heart shall rejoice in your salvation.
[6] I will sing to the LORD,
because he has dealt bountifully with me.

Psalm 13 is a psalm of individual lament and disorientation. With *lectio divina,* we read and listen for the word or phrase that touches our heart. The psalmist captures the pain and frustration of disorientation in the following phrases, any of which may pull you into focus and prayer:

- How long, O LORD? Will you forget me forever? (v. 1a)
- How long must I bear pain in my soul? (v. 2a)
- How long must I have sorrow in my heart? (v. 2b)
- Consider and answer me, O LORD! (v. 3a)
- I am shaken. (v. 4b)

As we let one of these phrases or words become a part of us, we claim our feelings of disorientation. The psalmist expresses alienation, betrayal, challenge, anguish, petition, even despair. Psalm 13 is a psalm of lament that expresses our experience of a crisis with God. We pray to move from an absent God to a God of presence. We seek a God who hears our cry and shares in our anguish. Our prayer might be a plea to God to remember us and be with us.

While we have been waiting in darkness, our steadfast God never stops loving us. Sometimes we are unable to pray to what we perceive as an absent God. When we can eventually accept that God was present even though we felt God was absent, we pray: "I trusted in your steadfast love" (Ps 13:5). In communion with God we rest in whatever we are experiencing; we are held as we are whether in a place of orientation or disorientation.

Psalm 13 voices our experience of chaos, darkness, and tragedy, but it ends in a spirit of new orientation: "But I trusted in your steadfast love; my heart shall rejoice in your salvation" (v. 5). Even when we are anxious, we can learn to trust and remember God's "steadfast love." Trust in a loving God gives us consolation that helps us move out of our disoriented experience of God and life. Lamentation and suffering then slowly give way to a liberated, confident self, a new orientation.

Psalms of New Orientation

According to Walter Brueggemann, psalms of new orientation always begin in darkness. We do not know how to solve our problems or climb out of the pit. We are just barely hanging on. Then God surprises us with new life. We receive illumination and insight. We see God responding to our lament. We celebrate this new awareness in praise. We are filled with feelings of harmony, peace, and confidence because God has been with us in our pain and anguish.[8]

Psalm 30

¹ I will extol you, O LORD, for you have drawn me up,
and did not let my foes rejoice over me.
² O LORD my God, I cried to you for help,
and you have healed me.
³ O LORD, you brought up my soul from Sheol,
restored me to life from among those gone down to the Pit.

⁴ Sing praises to the LORD, O you his faithful ones,
and give thanks to his holy name.
⁵ For his anger is but a moment;
his favor is for a lifetime.
Weeping may linger for the night,
but joy comes with the morning.

⁶ As for me, I said in my prosperity,
"I shall never be moved."
⁷ By your favor, O LORD,
you had established me as a strong mountain;
you hid your face; I was dismayed.

⁸ To you, O LORD, I cried,
and to the LORD I made supplication:
⁹ "What profit is there in my death,
if I go down to the Pit?
Will the dust praise you?
Will it tell of your faithfulness?
¹⁰ Hear, O LORD, and be gracious to me!
O LORD, be my helper!"

¹¹ You have turned my mourning into dancing;
you have taken off my sackcloth
and clothed me with joy,
¹² so that my soul may praise you and not be silent.
O LORD my God, I will give thanks to you forever.

Psalm 30 is a psalm of new orientation. This psalm hints at
the darkness and suffering that went before, but it is filled with

joy and gratitude because God has brought restoration and heal-ing. When studying and praying *lectio divina* with this psalm, you may be stopped by a number of phrases:

- You have drawn me up. (v. 1a)
- You have healed me. (v. 2b)
- You brought up my soul from Sheol. (v. 3a)
- Give thanks. (v. 4b)
- Weeping may linger for the night, but joy comes with the morning. (5b, c)
- You had established me as a strong mountain. (v. 7a)
- Hear, O LORD, and be gracious to me! (v. 10a)
- You have turned my mourning into dancing. (v. 11a)
- I will give thanks to you forever. (v. 12b)

As we reflect on one of these phrases or a word from a phrase, we let a new orientation permeate our being.

In this phase our spirits rejoice and we again feel that life is joyful. We know God has saved us. We have experienced God's healing in our lives. Restoration is a time of remembering what God has done and offering thanks. We sense a new inner strength. God's graciousness changes the way we perceive life so much that we want to dance through life. All we want to do is sing praise to God and live out of a grateful heart.

Reading, meditating, and praying with Psalm 30 creates a renewed experience of God as liberator, savior, healer, life-giver, and restorer. Because we have experienced God's mercy we have a new orientation. With the psalmist we experience life in a new way. We know what it is to be liberated, healed, and restored from anger, greed, despair, hatred, and the desire for retribution. We celebrate the transforming actions of a God who helps us to experience joy in life. We feel safe and secure, and for this we are thankful. We commit ourselves to living out of this new orienta-tion. We become joy-filled, confident people. Secure in God, we face life with a renewed confidence and trust.

Using *Lectio Divina* in a Group

Another way of entering into *lectio divina* is in the context of a group. The development of *lectio* as a group process originated in some of the base Christian communities in the Third World and has been adapted in many ways. Preparation, reading, meditation, prayer, contemplation, and action are all part of group *lectio*. In many ways the group process is much like praying *lectio* on one's own. There is a leader to guide the process, and there are opportunities to share how God has blessed you. It is powerful to experience God's stillness and goodness in the context of a group.

Preparation

You are invited to quiet your body, mind, and spirit. Ask yourself what will help bring you fully into this moment. Pay attention to your breathing. As you breathe in, invite the Spirit to open you and help you be receptive to God's Word. As you breathe out, let go of anything that keeps you from truly hearing the gifts of insight from the Holy Spirit. As you breathe in, feel the light of the Spirit surrounding your mind, heart, and whole body. As you breathe out, let go of anything that keeps you from being present to the scripture. Invite the Spirit to guide you during this session. Choose a short passage about five lines long.

Hear the Word Addressed to You

The first time the section is read, the leader will read it out loud slowly once or twice. Listen for the phrase or image God is inviting you to hear. Repeat it to yourself softly for one or two minutes. When the leader gives the signal, you may share with the group what you have received, or pass.

Hear the Word Addressed to Your Life

The second time the section is read out loud, focus on how your life is touched by the phrase or image God gave you. For about two to five minutes, attend to the sensory impressions or images that emerge, asking yourself, I hear....I see....I sense....I perceive....You might like to use reflection questions such as: *"Where does the content of this reading touch my life today?"*[9] Or, *"Where does this passage touch my life, my community, my nation, or my world today?"*[10] You may share your experience with the group or pass.

Hear the Word as an Invitation

The third time, listen for an invitation that you might apply to your life right now. Listen to the reading and spend from two to five minutes reflecting on the invitation from the word, phrase, or image that spoke to you. You might ask yourself a question such as the following: "What is God inviting me to be or do, or to change in my life?" You may want to reflect on the following phrase: "I believe God is...," and then share your experience with the group, or pass.

Pray

The group may choose to pray out loud, or in silence, or a combination of both. The prayer may extend outward to one another, the local community, or global community.

Conclusion

Scripture is always the foundation for praying *lectio divina* in a monastic way. The practice includes reading, meditating, praying, and acting on the Word of God. *Lectio divina* gives us an opportunity to be open to God's presence through the various rhythms of life: orientation, disorientation, and new orientation. *Lectio* nourishes us and guides us through life; study gives us greater insight about how we might live. We are invited to let scripture so permeate our being that we become living incarnations of God's Word. If we act on the wisdom we have acquired, we become a living prayer and all of life becomes the "work of God" (RB 52.5).

Practical Applications

- Slowly read aloud a small portion of Psalm 8 (orientation), or Psalm 13 (disorientation), or Psalm 30 (new orientation).
- Notice the word, phrase, or image where God invites you to stop.
- Spend time savoring that word, phrase, or image.
- Notice if an emotion is stirred.
- Reflect on how the word, phrase, or emotion leads you to:
  √ Orientation: life is stable, balanced, safe, and orderly; God is faithful, stable, and good.
  √ Disorientation: life is chaotic, dark, and painful; God is absent or hidden.
  √ New orientation: life is dark, you are barely hanging on, and then God surprises you with new life. God responds to your lament, and you celebrate this new awareness with praise.
- Let your reflection lead you to respond to God and life.
- Pray in response to what stirred in you.

CHAPTER EIGHT

Shortened Lectio for Busy Days

Only a morsel [a verse or two] of scripture is offered so that you can savor its meaning and relish the passage. This tiny selection from the word of God is full of spiritual nutrition.
—Joyce Rupp, *The Cup of Our Life*[1]

This chapter focuses on a simple approach to *lectio divina*. It is designed for those who want spiritual nourishment and have limited time. It is possible to weave *lectio* into a day filled with many demands. As a note of encouragement, remember that *lectio divina* is about conscious prayer. Prayer is *not* measured by the number of minutes or words. *Lectio* is about drawing nearer to God through scripture. *Quality* is the goal rather than *quantity*.

A Simple, Short Way to Pray *Lectio*

Beginning the Day

Preparation for *lectio divina* may begin with an intention or a desire. You might begin by acknowledging the Holy Spirit: "Spirit, help me to be present to you." Or you may want to give voice to your longing: "Open my heart, God," or "Lord, open my soul." Then choose a short scripture verse that you would like to work with. We offer a list of verses for short *lectio* at the end of this chapter. As you progress in this practice, you can choose your own scripture verse or passage.

Your *lectio divina* may be a moment of reading, reflecting, or praying or a combination of these practices. Allow yourself to be drawn to whatever practice you need. Read the scripture you've chosen slowly out loud. What is God inviting you to hear or see? Is there a word, phrase, image, or emotion that speaks to your heart and invites you to linger? Use all of your senses. Say the words, hear the words, taste the words, smell the words, and feel the words. Relish them. If it is an image or feeling, tend it. Let it become a part of you. As you meditate on the text, focus on the feelings or insights that are meaningful. Pay attention to them. Be with them. Carry this sentence into your day by memorizing it, writing it on a card, or posting it in a conspicuous place, like your computer screen. Listen for God's invitation and try to express it through your actions. Even the smallest bit of scripture can continue to unfold and nurture you throughout your day.

During the Day

Whenever you have a chance during the day, revisit the word, image, or emotion that spoke to your heart earlier. There are several ways to do this: say it out loud, think about it, picture it, feel it. Listen to how it speaks to you in the persons, events, or circumstances of the day. It may be that *lectio divina* is stirring a desire in you to act in some way. If there is a moment during the day when you are feeling stressed, inhale and exhale your breath-prayer. Invite God to tend to you and extend this care to anyone who comes into your presence. Remember God's presence is *always* with you. You need only respond, and practicing *lectio divina* is a way of being more responsive.

Ending the Day

Conclude the day with any of the following: using a breath-prayer, repeating a word out loud or silently, or focusing on an image or feeling that nurtured you during the day. Reflect on how this *lectio divina* befriended you. How did it influence your actions? Perhaps it offered you some wisdom about dealing with a person, event, or circumstance. Perhaps it warmed and expanded your heart or helped you stay connected with God and others during the day. Spend a short amount of time praying with your *lectio divina* experience. Express your gratitude to God or simply rest in God's presence. You may want to record the scripture verse, phrase, word, image, feeling, reflection, or prayer in your journal. You might like to draw, sing, or dance your prayer, or just hold the experience in your memory.

Another Simple Way to Pray *Lectio Divina* by *Sr. Dorothy Robinson, OSB*

Reading

Listen to the Word of God with the ear of your heart.

Meditation

Ponder God's Word in your heart.

Prayer

Let your heart speak to God.

Contemplation

Rest in God.[2]

Conclusion

There are many options for doing *lectio divina* in simple and shortened ways. Here are the main steps: Begin with an intention, desire, or breath-prayer; read a verse or passage aloud; reflect on the word, phrase, image, feeling, or insight from scripture that is given to you. Then, allow the verse or verses to continue to nourish you all day and to be expressed in your life. Act on the wisdom of scripture. Remember to use the gift of all your senses in praying *lectio* and to rest in your encounter with God. Over time, even this short and simple experience of *lectio divina* will lead you to a deeper, more intimate relationship with God and life.

Practical Applications

Beginning the Day

- Pray: "Spirit, help me to be present to you."
- Read the scripture verse or verses aloud slowly, several times.
  - √ Use all your senses: speak, hear, taste, smell, and feel the words.
  - √ Pay attention to the word, phrase, image, or feeling that speaks to your heart and invites you to linger.
- Savor, chew, and digest what you have read.
  - √ Linger with the word, phrase, feeling, image, or insight that speaks to your heart.
  - √ Tend it. Pay attention to it.
  - √ Assimilate it. Let it become a part of you. Relish it.
  - √ Memorize whatever speaks to your heart.
  - √ Carry the words into your day by memorizing the phrase, writing it on a card, or posting it in a place where you'll see it often, like your computer screen.
  - √ Listen for God's invitation and put it into action during the day.

During the Day

- Say aloud or think about the word, phrase, image, or feeling that spoke to your heart in your *lectio divina* time.
- Inhale and exhale a breath-prayer.
- Remember God's presence is always with you.
- Act on your *lectio divina*.
- Invite God to care for you and extend this caring to anyone who comes into your presence.
  - √ Listen to how God's Word speaks to you through persons, events, or circumstances.
  - √ Respond to the movements of your heart.

Concluding the Day

- Repeat the word, phrase, feeling, or image aloud that you focused on during the day.
- Reflect on how *lectio divina* befriended you today.
  - √ How did the wisdom of *lectio* extend to persons, events, or circumstances?
  - √ How did *lectio* help you stay connected with God and others?
  - √ How did *lectio* expand and fuel your heart?
- Spend a short amount of time praying with your *lectio divina* experience.
- Dialogue with God about what *lectio divina* revealed to you this day.
- Speak to God spontaneously in gratitude, petition, thanksgiving, joy, grief, anger, fear, compassion, or any feeling that is within you.
- Choose to record the scripture verse, phrase, word, image, feeling, reflection, or prayer in your journal.
- Write or draw your prayer.
- Rest in God's presence in silence without any words, images, feelings, or sensations. Just be in communion with God.
- Hold the experience in your memory.

Short *Lectio* Scripture Verses

Abide

"Those who abide in me and I in them bear much fruit, because apart from me you can do nothing." (John 15:5b)

"If you abide in me, and my words abide in you, ask for whatever you wish, and it will be done for you." (John 15:7)

Bless

Come, bless the LORD, all you servants of the LORD, who stand by night in the house of the LORD! Lift up your hands to the holy place, and bless the LORD. May the LORD, maker of heaven and earth, bless you from Zion. (Ps 134:1–3)

Every day I will bless you, and praise your name forever and ever. (Ps 145:2)

All your works shall give thanks to you, O LORD, and all your faithful shall bless you. (Ps 145:10)

My mouth will speak the praise of the LORD, and all flesh will bless [God's] holy name forever and ever. (Ps 145:21)

Blessed be the God and Father of our Lord Jesus Christ, the Father of mercies and the God of all consolation, who consoles us in all our affliction, so that we may be able to console those who are in any affliction with the consolation with which we ourselves are consoled by God. (2 Cor 1:3–4)

Blessed be the God and Father of our Lord Jesus Christ, who has blessed us in Christ with every spiritual blessing in the heavenly places, just as [God] chose us in Christ before the foundation of the world to be holy and blameless before [God] in love. (Eph 1:3–4)

Called, Chosen

I call upon you, O LORD; come quickly to me; give ear to my voice when I call to you. (Ps 141:1)

Do not fear, for I have redeemed you; I have called you by name, you are mine. (Isa 43:1)

"You did not choose me but I chose you." (John 15:16)

Compassion

The LORD is good to all, and [God's] compassion is over all that [God] has made. (Ps 145:9)

Can a woman forget her nursing child, or show no compassion for the child of her womb? Even these may forget, yet I will not forget you. (Isa 49:15)

Delight

I delight in the way of your decrees as much as in all riches. (Ps 119:14)

"My soul magnifies the Lord, and my spirit rejoices in God my Savior." (Luke 1:46–47)

Yet day after day they seek me and delight to know my ways. (Isa 58:2)

Who is a God like you, pardoning iniquity and passing over the transgression of the remnant of your possession? [God] does not retain [God's] anger forever, because [the merciful One] delights in showing clemency. (Mic 7:18)

Desire

Take delight in the LORD, and [God] will give you the desires of your heart. (Ps 37:4)

Then they were glad because they had quiet, and [God] brought them to their desired haven. (Ps 107:30)

You open your hand, satisfying the desire of every living thing. (Ps 145:16)

[God] fulfills the desire of all who fear [God]; [God] also hears their cry, and saves them. (Ps 145:19)

Discernment

"A spirit glided past my face; the hair of my flesh bristled. It stood still, but I could not discern its appearance. A form was before my eyes; there was silence, then I heard a voice: 'Can mortals be righteous before God? Can human beings be pure before their Maker?'" (Job 4:15–17)

To one is given through the Spirit the utterance of wisdom, and to another the utterance of knowledge according to the same Spirit, to another faith by the same Spirit, to another gifts of healing by the one Spirit, to another the working of miracles, to another prophecy, to another the discernment of spirits, to another various kinds of tongues, to another the interpretation of tongues. All these are activated by one and the same Spirit, who allots to each one individually just as the Spirit chooses. (1 Cor 12:8–11)

Faith

When Jesus heard [the centurion], he was amazed and said to those who followed him, "Truly I tell you, in no one in Israel have I found such faith." (Matt 8:10)

Then Jesus answered [the Canaanite woman], "Woman, great is your faith! Let it be done for you as you wish." And her daughter was healed instantly. (Matt 15:28)

[Jesus] said to her, "Daughter, your faith has made you well; go in peace." (Luke 8:48)

Faithfulness

Your steadfast love, O LORD, extends to the heavens, your faithfulness to the clouds. (Ps 36:5)

I have not hidden your saving help within my heart, I have spoken of your faithfulness and your salvation; I have not concealed your steadfast love and your faithfulness from the great congregation. (Ps 40:10–11)

I will thank you forever, because of what you have done. In the presence of the faithful I will proclaim your name, for it is good. (Ps 52:9)

Steadfast love and faithfulness will meet; righteousness and peace will kiss each other. (Ps 85:10)

But you, O LORD, are a God merciful and gracious, slow to anger and abounding in steadfast love and faithfulness. (Ps 86:15)

Fear, Terror

Even though I walk through the darkest valley, I fear no evil; for you are with me; your rod and your staff—they comfort me. (Ps 23:4)

The LORD is my light and my salvation; whom shall I fear? The LORD is the stronghold of my life; of whom shall I be afraid? (Ps 27:1)

But you indeed are awesome! Who can stand before you when once your anger is roused? From the heavens you uttered judgment; the earth feared and was still. (Ps 76:7–8)

Gratitude, Thanksgiving

Sing praise to the LORD, O you [God's] faithful ones, and give thanks to [God's] holy name. (Ps 30:4)

We give thanks to you, O God; we give thanks; your name is near. People tell of your wondrous deeds. (Ps 75:1)

Then [Jesus] took a cup, and after giving thanks, he gave it to them saying, "Drink from it, all of you; for this is my blood of the covenant, which is poured out for many for the forgiveness of sins." (Matt 26:27–28)

I do not cease to give thanks for you as I remember you in my prayers. (Eph 1:16)

May you be made strong with all the strength that comes from [God's] glorious power, and may you be prepared to endure everything with patience, while joyfully giving thanks to the

Father, who has enabled you to share in the inheritance of the saints in the light. (Col 1:11–12)

And all the angels stood around the throne and around the elders and the four living creatures, and they fell on their faces before the throne and worshiped God, singing, "Amen! Blessing and glory and wisdom and thanksgiving and honor and power and might be to our God forever and ever! Amen." (Rev 7:11–12)

Greed

Such is the end of all who are greedy for gain; it takes away the life of its possessors. (Prov 1:19)

All day long the wicked covet, but the righteous give and do not hold back. (Prov 21:26)

Groaning

We know that the whole creation has been groaning in labor pains until now; and not only the creation, but we ourselves, who have the first fruits of the Spirit, groan inwardly while we wait for adoption, the redemption of our bodies. (Rom 8:22–23)

For in this tent we groan, longing to be clothed with our heavenly dwelling. (2 Cor 5:2)

Growth

I planted, Apollos watered, but God gave the growth. So neither the one who plants nor the one who waters is anything, but only God who gives the growth. (1 Cor 3:6–7)

For now we see in a mirror, dimly, but then we will see face to face. Now I know only in part; then I will know fully, even as I have been fully known. (1 Cor 13:12)

"Let both of them grow together [weeds and wheat] until the harvest; and at harvest time I will tell the reapers, Collect the weeds first and bind them in bundles to be burned, but gather the wheat into my barn." (Matt 13:30)

Happiness

O taste and see that the LORD is good; happy are those who take refuge in [God]. (Ps 34:8)

Happy is everyone who fears the LORD, who walks in [God's] ways, You shall eat the fruit of the labor of your hands; you shall be happy, and it shall go well with you. (Ps 128:1–2)

Happy are the people to whom such blessings fall; happy are the people whose God is the LORD. (Ps 144:15)

Happy are those who find wisdom, and those who get understanding, for her income is better than silver, and her revenue better than gold. (Prov 3:13–14)

Those who are attentive to a matter will prosper, and happy are those who trust in the LORD. (Prov 16:20)

Hearing, Listening

Hear, O LORD, when I cry aloud, be gracious to me and answer me! (Ps 27:7)

Incline your ear, and come to me; listen, so that you may live. I will make with you an everlasting covenant, my steadfast, sure love for David. (Isa 55:3)

Hear my cry, O God; listen to my prayer. (Ps 61:1)

Heart

Prove me, O Lord, and try me; test my heart and mind. (Ps 26:2)

"Come," my heart says, "seek [God's] face!" Your face, LORD, do I seek. (Ps 27:8)

Wait for the LORD; be strong, and let your heart take courage; wait for the LORD! (Ps 27:14)

The counsel of the LORD stands forever, the thoughts of [God's] heart to all generations. (Ps 33:11)

[God] fashions the hearts of them all, and observes all their deeds. (Ps 33:15)

Create in me a clean heart, O God, and put a new and right spirit within me. (Ps 51:10)

My heart is steadfast, O God, my heart is steadfast. I will sing and make melody. (Ps 57:7)

From the end of the earth I call to you, when my heart is faint. Lead me to the rock that is higher than I. (Ps 61:2)

Let the oppressed see it and be glad; you who seek God, let your hearts revive. (Ps 69:32)

My flesh and my heart may fail, but God is the strength of my heart and my portion forever. (Ps 73:26)

When the cares of my heart are many, your consolations cheer my soul. (Ps 94:19)

With my whole heart I seek you; do not let me stray from your commandments. I treasure your word in my heart, so that I may not sin against you. (Ps 119:10–11)

A new heart I will give you, and a new spirit I will put within you; and I will remove from your body the heart of stone and give you a heart of flesh. (Ezek 36:26)

"Blessed are the pure in heart, for they will see God." (Matt 5:8)

"For where your treasure is, there your heart will be also." (Matt 6:21)

"Do not let your hearts be troubled. Believe in God, believe also in me." (John 14:1)

Hope

Truly the eye of the LORD is on those who fear him, on those who hope in [God's] steadfast love. (Ps 33:18)

"For there is hope for a tree, if it is cut down, that it will sprout again, and that its shoots will not cease. Though its roots grows old in the earth, and its stump dies in the ground, yet at the scent of water it will bud and put forth branches like a young plant." (Job 14:7–9)

Hospitality

"Come, you that are blessed by my Father, inherit the kingdom prepared for you from the foundation of the world; for I was hungry and you gave me food, I was thirsty and you gave me something to drink, I was a stranger and you welcomed me, I was naked and you gave me clothing, I was sick and you took care of me, I was in prison and you visited me." (Matt 25:34–36)

Be hospitable to one another without complaining. Like good stewards of the manifold grace of God, serve one another with whatever gift each of you has received. (1 Pet 4:9–10)

Humility

The fear of the LORD is instruction in wisdom, and humility goes before honor. (Prov 15:33)

You who are younger must accept the authority of the elders. And all of you must clothe yourselves with humility in your dealings with one another. (1 Pet 5:5)

"You yourselves know how I lived among you the entire time from the first day that I set foot in Asia, serving the Lord with all humility and with tears, enduring the trials that came to me." (Acts 20:18–19)

Jealousy

How long, O LORD? Will you be angry forever? Will your jealous wrath burn like fire? (Ps 79:5)

For jealousy arouses a husband's fury, and he shows no restraint when he takes revenge. He will accept no compensation, and refuses a bribe no matter how great. (Prov 6:34–35)

It stretched out the form of a hand, and took me by a lock of my head; and the spirit lifted me up between earth and heaven, and brought me in visions of God to Jerusalem, to the entrance of the gateway of the inner court that faces north, to the seat of the image of jealousy, which provokes to jealousy. (Ezek 8:3)

Joy

Weeping may linger for the night, but joy comes with the morning. (Ps 30:5)

Make a joyful noise to God, all the earth; sing the glory of [God's] name; give to [God] glorious praise. (Ps 66:1–2)

Your decrees are my heritage forever; they are the joy of my heart. (Ps 119:111)

The LORD, your God, is in your midst....[The holy one] will rejoice over you with gladness, [God] will renew you in [God's] love. (Zeph 3:17)

Rejoice in the Lord always; again I will say, Rejoice. Let your gentleness be known to everyone. (Phil 4:4–5)

"I have said these things to you so that my joy may be in you, and that your joy may be complete." (John 15:11)

"Ask and you will receive, so that your joy may be complete." (John 16:24)

Justice, Righteousness

My mouth will tell of your righteous acts, of your deeds of salvation all day long, though their number is past my knowledge. (Ps 71:15)

Give justice to the weak and the orphan; maintain the right of the lowly and the destitute. Rescue the weak and the needy; deliver them from the hand of the wicked. (Ps 82:3–4)

Righteousness and justice are the foundation of your throne; steadfast love and faithfulness go before you. (Ps 89:14)

All the words of my mouth are righteous; there is nothing twisted or crooked in them. They are all straight to one who understands and right to those who find knowledge. (Prov 8:8–9)

To do righteousness and justice is more acceptable to the LORD than sacrifice. (Prov 21:3)

Maintain justice, and do what is right, for soon my salvation will come, and my deliverance be revealed. (Isa 56:1)

Lament

Blessed be the LORD, for he has heard the sound of my pleadings. The LORD is my strength and my shield; in [God] my heart trusts. So I am helped, and my heart exults, and with my song I give thanks to [God]. (Ps 28:6–7)

You have seen, O LORD; do not be silent! O LORD, do not be far from me! Wake up! Bestir yourself for my defense, for my cause, my God and my LORD. (Ps 35:22–23)

Vindicate me, O God, and defend my cause against an ungodly people; from those who are deceitful and unjust deliver me! (Ps 43:1)

Insults have broken my heart, so that I am in despair. I looked for pity, but there was none; and for comforters, but I found none. (Ps 69:20)

Out of the depths I cry to you, O LORD. LORD, hear my voice! Let your ears be attentive to the voice of my supplication! (Ps 130:1–2)

But as for you, have no fear, my servant Jacob, says the LORD, and do not be dismayed, O Israel; for I am going to save you from far away, and your offspring from the land of their captivity. Jacob shall return and have quiet and ease, and no one shall make him afraid. (Jer 30:10)

Longing

O LORD, all my longing is known to you; my sighing is not hidden from you. My heart throbs, my strength fails me; as for the light of my eyes—it also has gone from me. (Ps 38:9–10)

As a deer longs for flowing streams, so my soul longs for you, O God. My soul thirsts for God, for the living God. When shall I come and behold the face of God? (Ps 42:1–2)

How lovely is your dwelling place, O LORD of hosts! My soul longs, indeed it faints for the courts of the LORD; my heart and my flesh sing for joy to the living God. (Ps 84:1–2)

Love

I will exult and rejoice in your steadfast love, because you have seen my affliction; you have taken heed of my adversities, and have not delivered me into the hand of the enemy; you have set my feet in a broad place. (Ps 31:7–8)

Let your face shine upon your servant; save me in your steadfast love. (Ps 31:16)

I am like a green olive tree in the house of God. I trust in the steadfast love of God forever and ever. (Ps 52:8)

When I thought, "My foot is slipping," your steadfast love, O LORD, held me up. (Ps 94:18)

For as the heavens are high above the earth, so great is [God's] steadfast love toward those who fear [God]. (Ps 103:11)

It is in vain that you rise up early and go late to rest, eating the bread of anxious toil; for [God] gives sleep to [God's] beloved. (Ps 127:2)

Love is patient; love is kind; love is not envious or boastful or arrogant or rude. It does not insist on its own way; it is not irritable or resentful; it does not rejoice in wrongdoing, but rejoices in the truth. It bears all things, believes all things, hopes all things, endures all things. (1 Cor 13:4–7)

Love never ends....And now faith, hope, and love abide, these three; and the greatest of these is love. (1 Cor 13:8, 13)

Above all, clothe yourselves with love, which binds everything together in perfect harmony. (Col 3:14)

Meditate

Let the words of my mouth and the meditation of my heart be acceptable to you, O LORD, my rock and my redeemer. (Ps 19:14)

My mouth shall speak wisdom; the meditation of my heart shall be understanding. (Ps 49:3)

I will meditate on your precepts, and fix my eyes on your ways. (Ps 119:15)

My eyes are awake before each watch of the night, that I may meditate on your promise. (Ps 119:148)

Mercy

Let your mercy come to me, that I may live; for your law is my delight. (Ps 119:77)

Have mercy upon us, O LORD, have mercy upon us, for we have had more than enough of contempt. (Ps 123:3)

The LORD is gracious and merciful, slow to anger and abounding in steadfast love. (Ps 145:8)

Patience

Let love be genuine; hate what is evil, hold fast to what is good; love one another with mutual affection; outdo one another in showing honor. Do not lag in zeal, be ardent in spirit, serve the Lord. Rejoice in hope, be patient in suffering, persevere in prayer. (Rom 12:9–12)

Be patient, therefore, beloved, until the coming of the Lord. The farmer waits for the precious crop from the earth, being patient with it until it receives the early and the late rains. You also must be patient. Strengthen your hearts, for the coming of the Lord is near. (Jas 5:7–8)

Peace

I will both lie down and sleep in peace; for you alone, O LORD, make me lie down in safety. (Ps 4:8)

May the LORD give strength to [God's] people! May the LORD bless [God's] people with peace! (Ps 29:11)

Depart from evil, and do good; seek peace, and pursue it. (Ps 34:14)

Let me hear what God the LORD will speak, for [the merciful One] will speak peace to [God's] people, to [God's] faithful, to those who turn to [God] in their hearts. (Ps 85:8)

[God] grants peace within your borders; [God] fills you with the finest of wheat. (Ps 147:14)

"Blessed are the peacemakers, for they will be called children of God." (Matt 5:9)

"Peace I leave with you; my peace I give to you. I do not give to you as the world gives. Do not let your hearts be troubled, and do not let them be afraid." (John 14:27)

"I have said this to you, so that in me you may have peace. In the world you face persecution. But take courage; I have conquered the world!" (John 16:33)

Therefore, since we are justified by faith, we have peace with God through our Lord Jesus Christ, through whom we have obtained access to this grace in which we stand; and we boast in our hope of sharing the glory of God. (Rom 5:1–2)

Refuge

You are indeed my rock and my fortress; for your name's sake lead me and guide me, take me out of the net that is hidden for me, for you are my refuge. Into your hand I commit my spirit; you have redeemed me, O LORD, faithful God. (Ps 31:3–5)

[God] drew me up from the desolate pit, out of the miry bog, and set my feet upon a rock, making my steps secure. (Ps 40:2)

But the LORD has become my stronghold, and my God the rock of my refuge. (Ps 94:22)

Rest

I lie down and sleep; I wake again, for the LORD sustains me. (Ps 3:5)

O my God, I cry by day, but you do not answer; and by night, but find no rest. (Ps 22:2)

O God, do not keep silence; do not hold your peace or be still, O God! (Ps 83:1)

Happy are those whom you discipline, O LORD, and whom you teach out of your law, giving them respite from days of trouble, until a pit is dug for the wicked. (Ps 94:12–13)

Or why was I not buried like a stillborn child, like an infant that never sees the light? There the wicked cease from troubling, and there the weary are at rest. (Job 3:16–17)

Stand at the crossroads, and look, and ask for the ancient paths, where the good way lies; and walk in it, and find rest for your souls. (Jer 6:16)

Search

I commune with my heart in the night; I meditate and search my spirit. (Ps 77:6)

O LORD, you have searched me and known me. You know when I sit down and when I rise up; you discern my thoughts from far away. You search out my path and my lying down, and are acquainted with all my ways. (Ps 139:1–2)

"And you, my son Solomon, know the God of your father, and serve [God] with single mind and willing heart; for the LORD searches every mind, and understands every plan and thought." (1 Chr 28:9)

Seek

Seek the LORD while [God] may be found, call upon [the merciful One] while [God] is near. (Isa 55:6)

They will receive blessing from the LORD, and vindication from the God of their salvation. Such is the company of those who seek [God], who seek the face of the God of Jacob. (Ps 24:5–6)

One thing I asked of the LORD, that will I seek after: to live in the house of the LORD all the days of my life, to behold the beauty of the LORD, and to inquire in [God's] temple. (Ps 27:4)

I sought the LORD, and he answered me, and delivered me from all my fears. (Ps 34:4)

Shelter

In the shelter of your presence you hide them from human plots: you hold them safe under your shelter from contentious tongues. (Ps 31:20)

You who live in the shelter of the Most High, who abide in the shadow of the Almighty, will say to the LORD, "My refuge and my fortress: my God, in whom I trust."(Ps 91:1–2)

Silence and Stillness

Be still before the LORD, and wait patiently for [God]; do not fret over those who prosper in their way, over those who carry out evil devices. (Ps 37:7)

I am silent; I do not open my mouth, for it is you who have done it. (Ps 39:9)

Be still, and know that I am God! (Ps 46:10)

But I have calmed and quieted my soul, like a weaned child with its mother; my soul is like the weaned child that is with me. (Ps 131:2)

Sit in silence, and go into darkness. (Isa 47:5)

Thanksgiving

See Gratitude.

Unity

How very good and pleasant it is when kindred live together in unity! (Ps 133:1)

I therefore, the prisoner in the Lord, beg you to lead a life worthy of the calling to which you have been called, with all humility and gentleness, with patience, bearing with one another in love, making every effort to maintain the unity of the Spirit in the bond of peace. (Eph 4:1–3)

The gifts [Christ] gave were that some would be apostles, some prophets, some evangelists, some pastors and teachers, to equip the saints for the work of ministry, for building up the body of Christ, until all of us come to the unity of the faith and of the knowledge of the Son of God, to maturity, to the measure of the full stature of Christ. (Eph 4:11–13)

Way of God and Guidance

Teach me your way, O LORD, that I may walk in your truth; give me an undivided heart to revere your name. (Ps 86:11)

The LORD watches over the way of the righteous, but the way of the wicked will perish. (Ps 1:6)

Lead me, O LORD, in your righteousness because of my enemies; make your way straight before me. (Ps 5:8)

For I have kept the ways of the LORD, and have not wickedly departed from my God. (Ps 18:21)

"Make me to know your ways, O LORD; teach me your paths." (Ps 25:4)

Wisdom

My child, if you accept my words and treasure up my commandments within you, making your ear attentive to wisdom and inclining your heart to understanding...then you will understand the fear of the LORD and find the knowledge of God. (Prov 2:1, 2, 5)

My child, do not let these escape from your sight: keep sound wisdom and prudence, and they will be life for your soul and adornment for your neck. (Prov 3:21–22)

I, wisdom, live with prudence, and I attain knowledge and discretion. (Prov 8:12)

The teaching of the wise is a fountain of life, so that one may avoid the snares of death. (Prov 13:14)

The wise of heart is called perceptive, and pleasant speech increases persuasiveness. Wisdom is a fountain of life to one who has it, but folly is the punishment of fools. The mind of the wise makes their speech judicious, and adds persuasiveness to their lips. (Prov 16:21–23)

Wisdom is radiant and unfading, and she is easily discerned by those who love her, and is found by those who seek her. She hastens to make herself known to those who desire her. (Wis 6:12–13)

I learned both what is secret and what is manifest, for wisdom, the fashioner of all things, taught me. There is in her a spirit that is intelligent, holy, unique, manifold, subtle, mobile, clear, unpolluted, distinct, invulnerable, loving the good, keen, irresistible, beneficent, humane, steadfast, sure, free from anxiety, all-powerful, overseeing all, and penetrating through all spirits that are intelligent, pure, and altogether subtle. (Wis 7:21–23)

Word

Let your steadfast love come to me, O LORD, your salvation according to your promise. Then I shall have an answer for those who taunt me, for I trust in your word. (Ps 119:41–42)

You are my hiding place and my shield; I hope in your word. (Ps 119:114)

I wait for the LORD, my soul waits, and in [God's] word I hope. (Ps 130:5)

Indeed, the word of God is living and active, sharper than any two-edged sword, piercing until it divides soul from spirit, joints from marrow; it is able to judge the thoughts and intentions of the heart. (Heb 4:12)

Zeal

It is zeal for your house that has consumed me; the insults of those who insult you have fallen on me. (Ps 69:9)

The surviving remnant of the house of Judah shall again take root downward, and bear fruit upward; for from Jerusalem a remnant shall go out, and from Mount Zion a band of survivors. The zeal of the LORD of hosts will do this. (Isa 37:31–32)

CHAPTER NINE

Journaling, Making Art, and Praying with Art with Lectio

The journals are one part history, one part prayer, one part
confessional, one part meditation, one part storage facility,
one part discipline, one part hope. More than that, this is the
one place where my own life intersects with the ancient
traditions of the daily examen and confession. Where the
thanksgivings are expressed in some deep way and where
I discover blessings that have been hidden to me for years.
It is the place where reconciliation begins, and accountability
too, where promises made and promises broken are
somehow mingled together to produce life.
—Robert Benson in *Living Prayer*[1]

We have explored in depth the various "moments" or steps of *lectio divina*: reading, meditation, prayer, and contemplation. In this chapter we turn our attention to ways we can express our prayer in an outward form through journaling and the arts. Having a channel to express what is stirred during *lectio divina* can be a very valuable practice. In the second half of this chapter we also explore ways we can use *lectio divina* to pray with other sacred "texts" such as poetry, art, and music, created by both ourselves and other people. *Lectio divina* gives us a way to listen for the many ways that God is speaking to us in the world.

The Value of Journaling

The opening quote by Robert Benson points out the many ways that keeping a journal is rooted in the Christian tradition. The practice of writing in a journal connects us to the traditions of confession, meditation, praise, and lament. Journals are a safe space to explore what is happening inside of us. The act of writing itself is a form of prayer when it connects us with God. In a journal we can give voice to all the joys and struggles of our lives openly and honestly. Writing our prayers gives us a way to record what is happening in our inner world over time, so that we can notice places where we are stuck as well as patterns of growth and change. It assists us as we navigate our journey through life. It provides a way for us to explore our relationship with God and an opportunity to express our response to God.

Keeping a journal helps our mind stay focused and enables us to see how we are learning and growing in our relationship with God. The words *journal* and *journey* both come from the Latin word *diurnus,* which means "daily." The daily practice of journaling opens us up to self-knowledge and new insight; it can become a journey of discovery. We begin to notice the patterns of insight and growth that emerge from our prayer. Journaling can provide a map for listening deeply to God's guidance. Regular engagement with scripture forces us to face our gifts and limitations. Writing in a journal provides a container for our spiritual growth and self-knowledge. Spiritual growth is a continual process of unfolding that leads to transformation. We never fully arrive, but journaling helps us cultivate this journey and nurture places of growth.

Writing down our inner voices helps the thinking mind and the feeling heart become integrated and tangible through ink on paper. Journaling *takes* time but it also *gives* us time, time to be with God and with the longings of our heart. A regular practice of *lectio divina* and journaling can be a path toward transformation that leads to a new attitude and new life. Journaling can deepen our sense of the holiness of all of life. God wants the nourishment of the Word to sink in and remain with us. Journaling reinforces this process so that the Word of God becomes an integral part of our day.

Benedictine author and monastic Macrina Wiederkehr says journaling for her is a way of celebrating her prayer:

> I journal because it is one way of being present to the life that unfolds on my path each day. I journal because I am filled with thoughts that I must do something with, lest I explode with beauty or pain or yearning....I journal because it is a way of saving the graced moments that God gives to me to use in future letters that may be consoling to people in moments of discouragement, pain, or joy.[2]

Journaling gives us a consistent way to experience God's presence and to record moments of grace along the way. There are no specific rules for journaling; there is no one right way of doing it. It is a dynamic, not a static, endeavor. It is best to follow whatever method that opens your heart to a greater awareness of God's presence. Journaling provides us with an opportunity to express ourselves in our own unique way and to bring the whole of who we truly are before God.

Journaling can be helpful before, during, and after *lectio divina*. Before *lectio* it can help clear the mind of whatever is blocking your awareness of God. Write about what is burdening you or distracting you. The journal is a safe place to put your cares. You can use a journal while praying *lectio* as well. You might want to keep a journal and pen on your lap and take notes about what is stirring within you. If a significant image or question rises up in you, write it down or make a sketch and then go back to savor it in your imagination. Journaling is also a useful tool to use after doing *lectio divina*. The journal can be a place for you to explore what emerges during your prayer. It can be a record of the ways God has moved you and spoken to you.

Suggestions for Keeping a *Lectio Divina* Journal

First, buy or make a journal that feels inviting to you. If a very beautiful one is intimidating to you, then a simple, everyday notebook might work better. You can always individualize it with materials you enjoy. The idea is to have something that you will actually use. Some people keep their journal on the computer. Make sure your journal is in a safe place. Ask others you live with to respect your privacy. You need to be able to be as honest as possible when you journal. Several suggestions for using your journal with your prayer experience are listed below. Try as few or as many as you like.

- Write about what is in your heart as you approach your prayer time. Empty your mind onto the page so that God can fill you.
- Use your journal to record what is happening as you move through the moments of *lectio divina*.
- Notice the associations that arise for you and write them in your journal. For instance, do other sacred texts come to mind? Maybe you are reminded of theological themes, connections to figures from church history, liturgical themes, or other life experiences.
- Write about your sense of invitation from *lectio divina* and how you feel moved to respond.
- Describe your encounter with the sacred presence. Attend to the thoughts, feelings, memories, hopes, and yearnings that emerge.
- Write about the associations that surface during meditation. Make note of the sensations and images that are stirred within you and the ways you feel touched by God.
- Use the journal as a place to dialogue with God or yourself about what emerges for you during *lectio*. Write a letter about the things that distract you from an awareness of God. Reflect on your life and the ways you feel God's presence or absence.

- Wrestle with the difficult issues of your life before God. Express your deepest sorrow and anger at God. Write a prayer of lament in the tradition of the psalms.
- Conclude formal *lectio divina* prayer by copying the word or phrase you are attracted to in your journal. You might want to keep an ongoing record of these words and phrases so that you can see patterns in the ways God is calling you.
- Write a short prayer in response to your experience. Let your prayer expand from your own concerns to those of the wider community and even the earth itself.
- Write a prayer of praise expressing your deepest gratitude and joys.

Using a journal as you practice *lectio divina* has many benefits. The journal is a record of the ways God has led you and touched you. Often the sense of God's presence during prayer can feel so fleeting. Writing your prayers and responses helps you to hold onto those experiences and continue to nurture God's continuing revelation in your life. When you are discouraged, a journal entry can remind you of how God has walked with you and touched you. Benedictine Abbot Jerome Kodell, describes how a journal is a reminder to him of the many wonderful ways God speaks:

> The *lectio divina* journal is more a collection of the words that God speaks to me (primarily, but not only, in a time of prayerful reading): quotations from Scripture, the Fathers, other spiritual writings, and ultimately any kind of human word (novels, poems, banners, letters) that carries the transforming word of God in my life. These are collected as privileged words of God...directed personally to my heart, with the hope that what once was a vehicle for God's sanctifying and healing touch will remain important in my life and be a source of power again later on....The spiritual journal in this sense is rather a record of God's word to me than a record of my reflection on the word and its effect in my life.[3]

The journal can become the place where we express the very personal ways God has spoken to us. Writing in a journal is an act of faith: it shows we believe that God is speaking to us and working in our lives all the time.

Practical Applications

Journaling Before Lectio Divina

- Consider what is weighing on you or distracting you. Let it go.

Journaling While Praying Lectio Divina

- Keep your pen on your lap and make notes of what is stirring you. Look at the section in this chapter on suggestions for keeping a *lectio divina* journal.
- Record your word or phrase and any reflections you have.
- Write about what energized you during meditation.
- Write your prayer.

Journaling After Lectio Divina

- Record the invitation you received from God during prayer and how you acted upon it.

Examples of Journaling while Praying *Lectio Divina*

See the examples at the end of chapters 3, 4, and 5.

The Value of Making Art

In addition to journaling, art-making can be another valuable tool for working with the fruits of our prayer. Cultivating the arts as a spiritual practice is a way of freeing our imaginations and developing valuable skills for living in the world. We live at a time when our capacity for imagining is being thwarted by television programs, video games, and the voracious maw of the Internet that encourage us to tune out of life. These distractions teach us to become passive consumers rather than active imaginers. Art-making is an opportunity to engage our imaginations and develop the gift of imagining.

Art-making is incarnational; it engages us with the stuff of life. The heart of Christianity is the belief that God became flesh. Scripture celebrates acts of creation and art-making. Throughout the Hebrew Scriptures we encounter the vitality of creative expression as a means of celebrating God's faithfulness. Moses and the Israelites sing a song of gratitude when God liberates them from Egypt. Miriam dances with other women and plays her tambourine to celebrate this event (Exod 15:1–21). David proclaims his praise of God in front of the ark by dancing with abandon (2 Sam 6:14–15). The psalmists revel in the glory of God's creation and handiwork (Pss 19, 104) and exhort us to "Sing to the Lord a new song" (Pss 33, 96, 149). The quintessential song to God within Christian mysticism is said to be the Song of Solomon, which celebrates the senses. We are invited to relish images of "nard and saffron, calamus and cinnamon," as doorways to a sensual experience of the divine (Song 4:14). Such biblical imagery supports our use of the senses as a way to meet and praise God. The Israelites are not commanded to build an austere temple in Jerusalem; God tells them in detail how to build a sumptuous sanctuary (1 Chr 28:11–12). In the New Testament, Jesus proclaimed the kingdom of God through metaphor, symbol, and story. He used these tools to teach us and to nourish the imagination. Matter and the world of the imagination are vehicles for God's revelation. When we create with matter or images we are participating in that revelation.

The importance of creativity in Christianity is especially evident in worship. While some Christian communities have rejected the use of the arts, most have enriched the liturgy by using artistic expression to glorify God. Music, movement, gesture, symbol, sound, drama, architecture, color, and taste all come together to celebrate the mystery of God's presence. The Christian sacramental perspective affirms the power of the material world to reveal the presence and activity of God. The Christian community is shaped by these vibrant acts of embodied imagination. We are challenged to live out our faith creatively and sent forth to express our intimacy with God in our daily lives.

It is important for us to create a safe space to experience the delight and wonder of creative expression. There we can explore our inner world with paint, markers, collage, poetry, movement, words, and sound. When we use art-making as a form of prayer, we begin to discover God in the playful, joyful, and experimental places of our lives. God wants to mold us into creative beings; this imparts a profound dignity to us and our work in the world— *God said it was good!*

Letting go of judgments about what is "good" or "bad" art is essential for people just beginning to use art as prayer. A remarkable freedom often emerges when we surrender to the movement of the Holy Spirit and allow the Spirit to guide our prayer through art. We need to slowly loosen our tight grip and submit to a process greater than ourselves. The practice of art-making requires space and time: we need to slow down and give ourselves room to create. Engaging in the arts helps us to be present to the moment and see things more deeply. By using the arts as a spiritual practice we are making time for our relationship with God through the conscious act of creating. Through the arts we discover a divine presence that is not a static but an active force in our lives.

Art-making encourages curiosity and wonder. It is an act of respect for the deeper mysteries at work in the world and the multidimensionality of God. The arts do not work in a linear way; they don't answer questions about life with "straight lines." The arts point to the complexities and ambiguities of this world. They reveal truths to us and invite us to rely on intuition, not just on logic and analysis. The arts awaken and enliven us. Engaging in creative acts is an energizing activity. The experience of being fully present has been described as being in an altered state of awareness where we lose track of time. We become totally absorbed by what we are doing and yet fully present to each moment: we are fully alive.

Suggestions for Responding to *Lectio Divina* by Making Art

There are many wonderful, imaginative ways to create art as a response to *lectio divina*. We offer a few suggestions here to get started:

- Begin exploring an artistic approach to prayer with a set of colored pencils, pens, or paints. You'll need a pad of blank paper or you can use a blank page in your journal. After your *lectio* experience, take some time to explore in color and shape what moved you. There is no right or wrong way to do this: the purpose is exploration and play-fulness in prayer. Simply follow your own longings and inclinations without worrying about what the final form will look like. What color and shape does your prayer want to take today? Give yourself permission to be totally immersed in the creative act. Let go of any concerns about the outcome and enjoy the process. See where the Spirit takes your art-prayer.

- Make a simple collage in response to your *lectio divina* prayer. Collage can be a good form of expression for some-one just starting with the arts because there is no drawing involved. Simply take some magazines and flip through them. Resist the temptation to read the articles at this time. Collect images that resonate with your experience, or images you find challenging. Cut the images out with scissors or tear them gently and lay them down on the paper.

Use a glue stick to adhere them to the surface. Spend some time with the finished piece. Notice where you placed the different images in relationship to each other and what the finished collage brings up for you. You might want to journal about the feelings and thoughts that your collage evokes.

- Take a small lump of clay in your hands. Spend some time getting familiar with the texture. Roll it into a ball, smooth it out. Explore how the clay feels in your hand. Call to mind the image from scripture of God as a potter (Jer 18:1–6). Explore the ways God is shaping your life. Close your eyes and remember the invitation from your *lectio divina* prayer. Begin to form something with the clay that symbolizes the gift God gave you through *lectio* today.

- Create a prayer altar where you can slowly add the creations you have made in response to your prayers. Make a sacred space that honors the unfolding of your relationship with God. Keep the journal in this space and take time to write your response to the images you have made.

- Use a literary approach to express your experience of *lectio divina*. Take the word or phrase that called to you as well as the images, feelings, memories, and sense of invitation that came up for you. Create a poem. Poetry is simply condensed language, which forces you to be selective with the images you use so you can capture the essence of your experience. Sometimes working with a particular poetic form is helpful and provides structure for expression. Haiku is a simple form of poetry that uses three lines: five syllables in the first line, seven syllables in the second line, and five syllables in the third line. Experiment with creating a haiku poem that expresses what you experienced during *lectio divina*. Write the poem in your journal. Here is a haiku written by Benedictine oblate John Forman:

For Thy love given,
May we live in gratitude.
Grace returned to Thee.

- Consider music as another art form you might explore to express your prayers. Take the word or phrase you focused on during your *lectio divina* experience and create a simple chant or mantra you can sing throughout the day. It doesn't have to be fancy, just a simple steady note can add power to prayer. Your prayer time might have brought to mind a song you already know. Honor this gift from God by singing as much of it as you can remember.
- Let your body express your experience of prayer. Take some time to center yourself and notice if your body wants to move in a particular way. Is there a gesture you could use to embody your response to God's invitation? You might try combining a chant or mantra with a movement. Keep it simple: this is a way of connecting with your body in prayer.

Art-making helps us to explore prayer in a variety of ways. God speaks to us not only through rational thinking, but also through image and color and sound. Using the arts in prayer gives us access to another language to explore and express our relationship to the sacred.

Practical Applications

- Explore creative expression with paint, markers, collage, icons, poetry, movement, words, or sound.
- Follow your longings and see where they take your prayer.
- Look at other suggestions given earlier in this chapter in the section on responding to *lectio divina* with art-making.

Example of *Lectio Divina* with Romans 7:15 through Making Art —*by Cheryl Eiger*

I do not understand my own actions. For I do not do what I want, but I do the very thing I hate. (Rom 7:15)

The Value of Praying with Already-Created Art

The arts have long been celebrated by Christian tradition as a way of encountering the Holy One. Through art, we begin to see God's presence in the world more and more; as the previous section described it, art is incarnational. If we hold a sacramental vision, then we believe that God pulses in the world and that matter is not a barrier to the holy but a doorway.

Making art can be a profound response to *lectio divina*, but so can praying with art created by others. Simply think of well-known works of religious art, such as Michelangelo's *Pietà*, Bach's *Mass in B Minor*, or Rublev's *The Hospitality of Abraham*, his icon of the Trinity. These doorways to God lift up not only the artist, but also the viewer, the listener, as well.

Thus, as *lectio* deepens our vision of the sacred in everything, we discover there are many kinds of "texts" that can become doorways for us to greater intimacy with God. Here we offer some ways of practicing *lectio divina* with different kinds of sacred "texts," including the visual arts, poetry, music, movies, and motion.

Praying with Poetry: *Lectio Divina*

Poetry is language condensed and illuminated. When we read poetry written by other people, we are reading the same words we use for prose, but poetry has the potential to reveal the sacred to us in new ways. Poetry is full of compact images and it can often surprise us with unusual connections between images and ideas that lead to deeper understanding. Poetry enables us to see things we never expected to see. Much of scripture is written in a poetic form that makes use of metaphor, rhythm, meter, sound, and image to help us deepen our awareness of God. Praying with other people's poetry is probably the most straightforward application of *lectio divina* to the arts because we are praying with another written text.

There are many wonderful poets to choose from when doing *lectio divina*: Denise Levertov, Mary Oliver, David Whyte, Rainer

Maria Rilke, and Jalal ad-Din Muhammad Rumi, just to name a few. There are also many good anthologies of sacred poetry, and the list of further reading at the end of this book has more suggestions. Use any poem that evokes a sense of the holy for you.

Preparation

Before you begin, make sure you have allowed yourself enough time to enter deeply into this experience. It takes some time to move from the noise of the day to a place of utter stillness where you can listen deeply. Practice letting go by placing any worries or burdens in God's care. Take as much time as you need to turn inward and settle into stillness. Sit comfortably, shift your body so you feel relaxed and open. Use any technique that helps to quiet your mind and heart, such as focusing on your breath or chanting. Enjoy silence for a few moments. When you feel fully present and ready to listen to God's voice, move into the next moment.

Reading God's Word (Lectio)

Read the poem at least twice—aloud—the first time for familiarity, the second time to enter more deeply into the text. Savor each phrase and gather the words into your depths. Listen for a word or phrase that captures your attention, any word that shimmers, beckons, invites, or addresses you. It can also be something that you find unnerving, challenging, or unsettling. Watch for anything that seems to be especially ripe with meaning. Some days a word or phrase may jump right out at you. Other days there may be a much more subtle and gentle invitation. Listen until you have a sense of where the invitation dwells, then repeat the word to yourself in the silence and savor it.

Reflecting on God's Word (Meditatio)

Read the poem again and continue allowing the word or phrase to unfold in your memory and imagination. Let it work within you and speak even more deeply to your heart. Notice what feelings or images arise for you. Let the Spirit expand your capacity for listening and open you to a fuller experience of God's voice speaking through poetry. What do you see, hear, touch, or remember? What is evoked in you? Notice where this passage touches your life. Allow it to interact with your thoughts, your hopes, your memories, your desires. Rest in this awareness for some time.

Responding to God's Word (Oratio)

After a time you will be moved to a deeper insight that will evoke a desire to respond and say yes to God. When you are ready, read the poem again. Attend to the way the words connect with your life right now. How does the text relate to what you have heard and seen this day? How does it connect with what is happening at home, at work, and in your leisure time? Is God calling you to anything in your present circumstances? Is there a challenge presented here? Take an extended period of time to explore these questions and then respond to God in whatever way seems appropriate. Allow your whole being to respond in a prayerful dialogue. Express to God your honest thoughts, feelings, and desires. Let yourself be touched and changed by the Word of God. Give yourself time to rest with any new insights.

Resting with God's Word (Contemplatio)

Finally, simply relax in the presence of the One who has spoken to you lovingly and intimately. Allow yourself to simply *be* in God's presence. Let go of words and enjoy being still. Take in and receive all that God offers you in this moment. Rest in the silence of God's warm embrace and allow your heart to be moved with gratitude for this time of prayer. Stay in this loving space as long as you need.

Closing

Take a few moments to reflect on this experience. How did poetry speak to you as a sacred text? Were you willing to hear God's voice there? Let the text remain with you throughout the day and repeat it to yourself at various times. See what unfolds as you allow God to speak through poetry. If you are feeling especially moved by this experience, you might want to write your own poem in response. Do you need to express your pain or anger through poetry? How might you express your gratitude to God through a poem? What would a poem about your yes to God say?

Practical Applications

- Prepare yourself by sitting in a comfortable and relaxing position.
- Choose a poem.
- Read it aloud twice.
- Savor each phrase and gather the words into your depths.
- Listen for a word or phrase that captures your attention.
- Read the poem again and let the word or phrase unfold in your memory and imagination.
- What do you see, hear, touch, or remember?
- What is evoked in you?
- Notice where this passage touches your life.
- Allow your whole being to respond in a prayerful dialogue.
- Allow yourself to simply be in the silence of God's presence without words, thoughts, or images.

Example of *Lectio* Using Rachel Srubas's Poem "Ready Me to Respond" *by Noelle Rollins*

I have been using the same comfortable chair for my prayer-time for years. I have moved it to different places in my house and as it moves, I go with it. It doesn't seem to matter what room the chair is in; it is the chair itself that is my "prayer space."

I do my *lectio* in the morning after my kids have left for school and the house is quiet. I make myself a cup of coffee, light a candle next to my chair, and then I sit quietly and drink my coffee. This helps me to still my thoughts and get me focused on prayer-time.

Today I am using the following poem by Benedictine oblate Rachel M. Srubas, entitled "Ready Me to Respond."

Ready Me to Respond

In the beginning, you sighed.
You spoke over chaos and made the original day.
This day shines as that one must have done,
the sky a bright arc,
the earth a dark dynamic,
everywhere, beings you articulate in love.
When you speak, life pulses in my limbs.
I run with wild energy you breathe into me.

Your second word comes: a summons,
curbing the frenzy, guiding my feet.
Open the ear of my heart today.
Encourage me to do a harder thing
then mere hearing;
ready me to respond.

I'm fond of my internal monologue,
the sound of my mental soliloquy,
relevant to no one but me.

Obedience. The very word fences me in.
I chafe at the thought, and then—
find myself shaken awake
by some act of uncommon decency
or outrageous violation
that shouts me out of my self-
preoccupation and back
to the land of the living:

here, where you breathe
and name everything,
where my heart's ear bends
and my life depends
first on obedient listening.
—Rachel M. Srubas[4]

I read the poem three times, first silently to myself and then two times out loud. I pause in places when I feel particularly drawn to a word or phrase. I am not sure at first which one is calling to me so I read it over again until I settle on one particular word or phrase. I am not sure how this happens, but as I read the text over and over again I slowly become aware of which phrase is rising to the surface.

Today it is the line in the poem that is also the title: "Ready me to respond." After my heart has settled on a phrase, I journal. Some people sit quietly and meditate, I sit quietly and write. For me, I cannot meditate on the words unless my hand is writing. The act of writing helps my body to bring the words from the outside into my heart. It is just a simple free-write: I write down the things that just pop into my head about the phrase I have settled on. I don't try to think too much about what I am writing, I just let it flow out of my pen and onto the paper. Eventually my pen helps me find what my heart is seeking, what God is inviting me toward. Today during my journaling I found myself coming to this place: "God is inviting me to see 'how' I respond to the needs and calls around me—to look at my heart as I respond and see what is growing there—what fruit is falling from the trees and vines that make up my soul."

I always end my *lectio* and writing time with a written prayer. Today I wrote:

Loving Creator, the world edges in all around me; its needs seem overwhelming, more than I can handle. Lord, I pray, *Ready me to respond* without fear or laziness. *Ready me to respond* with a heart that bears loving and useful fruit. Show me how to step into this day alert, attentive, and ready for all that you might bring my way. Amen.

I end my prayer time with a few minutes of silence, blow out my candle saying "thank you," and then go about my day. I take my phrase or word with me so that it can continue to unfold in my heart and open new things up to me when I come into contact with people and events throughout the day.

Praying with Icons and Images: *Visio Divina*

St. John of Damascus (c. 676–749), a Syrian monk, wrote: "The invisible things of God since the creation of the world are made visible through images."[5] If we have a sacramental vision, then any image offers us an opening to the holy. Certain images, such as icons, have a privileged place as vehicles of revelation. Orthodox Christianity has a wonderful and ancient tradition of gazing upon icons as windows to God.

Icons are considered sacred "texts" in a more literal way than other images; in fact, the proper way to refer to the detailed and fixed ritual is not painting an icon, but *writing* one. An iconographer does not "paint a picture." Through divine inspiration, he or she "writes" a visual Gospel, and like the four Gospels, the *visual* Gospel of the icon brings an actual presence into the world.

Lectio divina is one way of entering into a contemplative experience with an icon. This way of praying with icons and images can be called *visio divina*, or "sacred seeing." When you use this way of praying, you'll want to select an icon or a sacred image that draws you. You may already have an icon in your home, or you can find them online. For example, an Eastern Orthodox monastic community in Wisconsin sells icons as part of their ministry; these range from inexpensive laminated prints to hand-painted reproductions. Their Web site is www.skete.com.

You may want to browse through their images and find one that speaks to you and invites you into prayer.

Preparation

You prepare to work with icons in much the same way as you do for scripture or poetry. Find a place where you will not be disturbed and take time to settle yourself into stillness. Get in touch with your breath and your body. Relish the silence. Draw your attention to this sacred time you have made for yourself. Be aware of your desire to grow in intimacy with God.

Gazing Upon the Image

The first moment in *lectio* is reading God's Word. Because the icon is an entirely different kind of sacred text, you need to enter into the experience in a different way.

Begin by exploring the entire image with your eyes. Notice the various colors and shapes, the different figures and symbols. Take time to let your eyes wander over the entire image. Look more deeply at the different sections of the icon. Notice the subtleties of shadow and expression. As you move your focus slowly around the image, pay attention to anything in particular about this icon that captures your attention. Be aware of any section that calls to you, challenges you, or invites you to deeper reflection. Let your eyes be drawn to this place and rest there. Take a few moments to absorb this experience and to really be present to the colors, shapes, figures, and symbols.

Reflecting on the Image

Now focus more deeply on the place in the icon that captured your attention. Let it draw you more deeply into the experience. Invite it to unfold in your imagination. Notice if it evokes any memories, feelings, or other images. Let the icon create spaciousness within you to hold whatever is stirring there. Become aware of what the icon touches in you.

Responding to the Image

After you have taken time to let your imagination work and your heart be touched, turn your focus to the ways you feel moved to respond. What is the invitation behind the images, memories, and feelings that unfolded for you? How is God speaking to your life through this icon? What is the "yes" within you that is longing to be expressed? Take some time to explore your responses through silence and/or journaling.

Resting with God

After you are in touch with the invitation being extended to you, begin to release all the words and images that have been flooding your heart. Our understanding of God is broadened through the image but ultimately it can never contain the fullness of God. Close your eyes for a few moments and savor the darkness and sense of surrender to the depth and breadth of God. Allow yourself some time to rest and simply *be*.

Closing

When you have reached the end of your prayer time, you may want to go back to the icon again and just gaze at it. Focus on the whole image this time. Notice if anything else leaps out. Offer a prayer of thanks for the gift of this time and for God's presence in beauty and stillness. After your time with the icon, you may want to explore your experience using art materials to express what happened in your prayer.

The experience of praying with icons and other images is quite different from praying with words. One form of prayer is no better than the other: visual prayer is simply another doorway to sacred awareness. For some people, praying with icons is quite challenging; for others, it is more comfortable than praying with words. Honor the prayer form that brings you closer to God and opens you to a sense of the holy presence that dwells within you.

Practical Applications

- Settle into stillness.
- Gaze upon the image.
- Explore the entire image with your eyes.
- Notice the various colors and shapes, the different figures and symbols.
- Focus slowly on anything in the image that captures your attention.
- Reflect on the part of the icon that captured your attention.
- Let it draw you more deeply into the experience.
- Invite it to unfold in your imagination and notice if it evokes any memories, feelings, or other images.
- Turn your focus to the ways you feel moved to respond.
- What is the invitation behind the images, memories, and feelings that unfolded for you?
- How is God speaking to your life through this icon?
- Release all the words and images that have been flooding your heart. Simply rest and be.

About Writing the Icons *Our Lady of Tenderness* and *Our Lady of Sorrows* by *Julie Barrett Ziegler*

For this *lectio*, I chose to work with two icons I have written as a commission for St. Michael Parish's Chapel of Repose in Olympia, Washington. The newly refurbished chapel holds the tabernacle that contains the reserved Eucharist for liturgy. These icons continue to work on my heart and my personal devotional life now, just as they did when they were being prayed into being in my studio. They are both very important spiritual images for me...and this was not always so. They are images of the same two people at very different times in the life they shared. The first is *Our Lady of Tenderness*, from a fourteenth-century image of the nativity of Christ, with the infant being held by his mother Mary. The companion icon is *Mater Dolorosa*, or *Our Lady of Sorrows*, from Golgotha.

These two icons work in quiet concert with the tabernacle, which is positioned between them, to express a full visual experience of the paschal mystery of Christianity. I have always loved the many images of Mary and Jesus as a baby. The depiction of a mother and her child are among the most ancient and most often-repeated images in world art. So, although I will describe *lectio* within the Christian idiom, this image also includes pre-Christian roots, such as Isis and Horus, Kore and her son Aeon, and others.

The more difficult image for me has been the pieta: the image of Mary embracing the body of her lifeless child. Anyone who has ever given birth or lost someone who was dear to them can relate to these archetypal images of birth and death as the most pivotal experiences of human life. These two images come together for me in a visual *lectio* prayer, which I share here.

An Example of *Lectio Divina* with the Icons of *Our Lady of Tenderness* and *Our Lady of Sorrows*, by Julie Barrett Ziegler

I enter the cold, quiet chapel, softly lit by the winter sun. The marble floor echoes my careful, solitary, slow footsteps. I stand before the tabernacle, where I look up to see both icons, as they hang on either side. The gold leaf cannot help but shine, even in this half-light. The deep rich colors draw me, invite me. I close my eyes. I breathe. I give thanks for this time. I begin. I open my eyes and LOOK. I am praying with my eyes, *looking*, not just quickly skimming, but really *looking*, remembering all the hours I sat with these wooden boards in my lap, cradling them like a small child...putting layer upon layer of soft color washes over the drawing...bringing the image "up" from the deepest shadows to the illuminated glow on their faces. A hundred hours or more I gave in the writing of these icons, and they are looking back at me, now.

Our Lady of Tenderness is young, beautiful, dressed as a royal queen, with a radiant, calm, soft smile upon her lips. She cradles her son, who looks up at her with love. Their cheeks touch, in the tenderness of intimacy, of new treasure, of belonging. Thirty-three jewels trim her embroidered crimson veil to symbolize the thirty-three years of earthly life she will share with her new son. Twelve fiery, flaming stars encircle her head, creating her halo, like a queen's crown. Her gaze is a soft, loving yes; it is tender, with love for her baby. They belong together. He is her treasure. She says, "Look upon my jewel, given into my keeping, proof of God's love for me, and for you." So many times, I remember cuddling my own babies, their soft cheek against my own, feeling so in love with them, marveling at the expansiveness of my love for them. Yes, this is what she feels, holding her son...the awesome, terrible, earth-shattering tenderness of unconditional love.

It is hard to turn away from this calm embrace of love to the second icon, but that is *lectio*, too: to have the courage to look upon that which would make us more than uncomfortable, that which convicts us into absolute personal honesty, honesty which is not afraid of death or change. The icon of *Mater Dolorosa, Our Lady of Sorrows,* is hard to look at. It was very difficult to write this icon. It depicts the moment when the dead Christ is laid in his mother's waiting arms at the foot of the cross. Again, she embraces her son, now grown to manhood, his earthly work finished, his eyes closed in death. Her dark blue mantel tells of her grief in this moment. I imagine her waiting, suffering the unspeakable with her child, wanting every second to take him down, to heal him, to help him...but I pause...this is how it is with children. My children were never mine...they were just given to me for safekeeping, for so short a time. I have watched my own be lifted up on crosses of their own making, as I stood helplessly by,

suffering with them, but not able to free them from their own life-paths. This is harder, so much harder, than giving birth and raising them. I am no less a mother, as I stand as witness.

This Mary is older, more gaunt, and somber—the blackened sun and the blood-red moon are above her. She is crying, and through her penetrating gaze, she seems to say, "Make your life worth this sacrifice. Make his life matter, and his death remembered, by how you live your own." There is no easy glancing at this image of the stark reality of mortal life, this gateway. Still, she brings tenderness that rises over this horrific event; still, her cheek caresses his. She is not afraid to hold him, to touch him, wounded and lifeless. I think: "How many times have I willingly caressed the death, or change, that came down from a cross, into my own arms?" Death doesn't stop a woman from being a mother, or a child from being a son, a daughter. These titles are sacred, they are *verb*, they are active and timeless. They have no end.

I pull myself away from her eyes and feel myself standing again on the cold marble floor, before the tabernacle: birth and death, and a golden chest between them. The Real Presence is the mystery, waiting to be received. The tabernacle is closed, its carved, golden doors hinting at the promise that lies within. Birth and death, and the promise within: it is the paschal mystery being shown before me. How many birthings and dyings and rebirths have I myself *embraced,* in gratitude for their gift, in my own mysterious journey back to the heart of God?

I bow, feeling tired but soft, filled with gratitude for the reminder that life is sacred and precious, and that our length of time here is mercifully unknown. I feel the echo of my prayer lingering there, as I pass through the doorway.

Praying with Music: *Audio Divina*

Many people of faith have valued music as a way of expressing one's humanity, as well as a way to glorify God. For example, the great classical composer Johann Sebastian Bach signed all of his musical compositions SDG, meaning *Soli Deo Gloria*, or "to the Glory of God alone."[6]

St. Hildegard of Bingen,[7] the twelfth-century Benedictine abbess, believed that music was an essential part of her community's formation. One example of her passion for music is seen at the end of her life when she was in conflict with church authorities over an excommunicated man who was buried on the grounds of her convent. As a result of the conflict, the entire convent was deprived of Mass, communion, and liturgical chant for six months. Hildegard was more upset about being forbidden to sing than being forbidden to receive communion. During her lifetime, she wrote a large volume of music for her community to use during the Divine Office, which is now known as the Liturgy of the Hours. In one of her antiphons she offers us a wonderful image of the sacred nature of music:

> To the Trinity be praise!
> God is music, God is life
> that nurtures every creature in its kind.
> Our God is the song of the angel throng
> and the splendor of the secret ways
> hid from all humankind,
> But God our life is the life of all.[8]

Music has an incredible power in our lives that originates perhaps from our heartbeat, that primordial life-sustaining rhythm. Have you ever heard a song you loved and played it over and over again? *Lectio divina* can offer us a life-giving way of praying more deeply with the music we love. Praying with music is a very different experience than praying with words or images. Praying in this way might be called *audio divina*, or "sacred listening."

Preparation

It is a good idea to choose music *without* words at first because words add another layer of meaning to the experience.

Praying with just the sounds of instruments gives you space to receive your own meaning from the prayer time. You might want to start with a recording of one of Bach's compositions, although any piece of music that you feel especially drawn to would be fruitful. Select a movement or a piece of music that lasts up to about five minutes. You will be playing it again and again, so keeping it brief will help you focus your prayer.

Prepare for your prayer by finding a quiet area and taking some time to settle into a place of silence and stillness. Breathe deeply and pay attention to how your body feels. Become aware of the sacredness of this time you have set aside to be present to God.

First Hearing

As in praying with icons, *lectio divina* with music needs to be approached differently because it is an entirely different kind of sacred "text." Play the piece of music once to enter into its landscape, then a second time to move more deeply into it. Notice the sounds of the notes and the silences between them. Release the movement of the music. Be present to how it rises and falls in your body and imagination. Allow the music to fill you. Breathe it in. Slowly become aware of any dominant sound, image, or feeling that is calling to you. Rest with that image or feeling, take it in, and be fully present to it.

Second Hearing

Play the music again. This time, hold the sound, image, or feeling that first called to you, and let it draw you more deeply into the experience. Allow it to unfold in your imagination and notice if any memories, feelings, images, or other melodies are evoked. Notice how the music touches you, and consider how you might express what you are feeling. Notice whether you feel any sense of the body wanting to move. Be aware of how the music is flowing through you. Notice what is being evoked.

Third Hearing

Play the music a third time. This time, focus on how your heart wants to respond. What invitation is present for you today in the unfolding of sounds, images, memories, and feelings? How is God speaking to your life in this moment, through this music? What is the yes within you that is longing to be expressed? If you feel comfortable singing (or even humming), take a moment to express with your voice what you are experiencing in your body. You can use a simple sound or line from the piece, a line from a song you know, or something you create in the moment.

Resting with God

Spend some time resting in silence and releasing the sounds, feelings, and images that are stirring inside. Close your eyes for a few minutes and rest in the awareness of God's presence. Allow yourself some time to simply *be*.

Closing

When you have come to the end of your prayer time you may want to play the music again and experience it anew. Notice if anything else stirs in you. Offer a prayer of thanks for the gift of this time and for God's presence in beauty and stillness. In response to your encounter with music you may want to use sound to explore what happened in your prayer experience. What does your yes to God sound like this day?

Practical Applications

- Choose a piece of music without words. Select a section of the piece. This could be anything from a musical phrase to an entire movement.
- Find a quiet area and settle into silence.

- Listen to the section twice.
- Notice the sounds of the notes and silences between them.
- Be present to how the music rises and falls in your body and imagination.
- Become aware of any dominant sound, image, or feeling that is calling to you.
- Listen to the section again. Hold the sound, image, or feeling that first called to you, and let it draw you more deeply into the experience.
- Allow it to unfold in your imagination and notice if any memories, feelings, images, or other melodies are evoked.
- Listen to the section again. Focus on how your heart wants to respond.
- Open yourself to whatever invitation is present for you today in the unfolding of sounds, images, memories, and feelings.
- Listen to how God is speaking to your life in this moment, through this music.
- Spend some time resting in silence and releasing the sounds, feelings, and images that are stirring inside.

Example of *Lectio Divina* with the Music of Hildegard of Bingen *by Jerry DeVore*

In the preparation phase, I sat at my dining room table while my wife watched football in the neighboring room. I created silence and a sacred place by putting on headphones and cultivating an intent towards musical prayer. I selected "A Vision," the title track from Richard Souther's production of Hildegard of Bingen's canticles. The song is about four minutes long. In the first hearing, the clutter of my mental life and the distractions in the background faded as I became receptive and absorbed in the music. In the second hearing, space opened and it seemed that an individual singer expressed deep longing as if reaching out to God, in a reverberating and resonant cathedral. Then she is joined by bass and xylophone, the roof opens, and the walls fall away to reveal the pinpoint lights of thousands of stars in a night sky. The stars come closer and the points expand into luminous forms and are revealed as angels. My eyes flowed with tears and I cried in exultation and joy. "Oh God" are the words that formed to express this inner sense of humility, joy, awe, and gratitude. In the closing phase, I reverberated with a sense of awe and connection with the divine. I sensed God as a vast presence and yet right here, deep inside me at the same time.

Praying with Movies: Film *Divina*

Praying with movies is another form of visual imagery that can be a vehicle for God's grace. Movies have become the storytellers of our time. They offer us images of the human journey that we share across culture and religious tradition, images that capture important truths. If we believe that God is in all of life, films can provide something that speaks to us and our lives about our own sacred story. God's glory within us, God's healing, and God's compassion can become more apparent when we reflect on how God speaks to us through "film *divina*."

In the film *Akeelah and the Bee*, Dr. Larabee believes learning is motivated by self-esteem. He encourages Akeelah with the words of Marianne Williamson: "Our deepest fear is not that we are inadequate. Our deepest fear is that we are powerful beyond measure....We were born to make manifest the glory of God that is within us."[9] In *The Horse Whisperer*, a teenage girl and her prized horse are wounded both physically and emotionally. The film "honors the spiritual practice of being present as the characters allow healing to proceed at a natural pace."[10] *Hotel Rwanda* is based on the true story of hotel manager Paul Rusesabagina, who saved his family and 1,200 refugees from the genocide that occurred in Rwanda in 1994. A description of the movie says, "At the urging of his wife, [Paul Rusesabagina] expands his circle of compassion to save his neighbors and even complete strangers.

He shows us what it means to cross over in a time when our world is experiencing staggering violence and divisions."[11]

Each year the magazine *Spirituality and Health* has an article that features "The Ten Most Spiritually Literate Films." The focus is on movies that enrich and inform our spiritual journey and our prayer life. If you prefer to work with a film that's known for its spiritual literacy, *Spirituality and Health* provides a variety of possibilities.

Preparation

Before you begin to do film *divina*, allow yourself to let go of anything which might keep you from being present to this viewing. Breathing and relaxing your body can help you transition into this film *divina*. When you feel relaxed and attentive, turn on the film.

Viewing the Film

As you view the film, pay attention to where you connect in a special way with a plot, an image, a character, a line in the film, a dialogue, a conversion moment, or a symbol. Replay in your mind the portion that speaks to you. Mentally slow the film down and let it connect with your heart and your experiences. Whether you are viewing a VHS tape or a DVD, it is possible to replay the section. Just allow yourself to be with whatever causes you to pause and wonder.

Reflecting on the Film

As you attend to whatever captures your attention, see what it evokes in you. If it is the plot, what about the plot speaks to your life? What emerges for you? If it is a character, what is it about the character that draws you? Does this character remind you of any portion of yourself? If it is a line from the film, spend time repeating and saying the line. If it is a piece of dialogue, ask yourself what insights are awakened in you? What do you discover in the dialogue that interlocks with your life? If it is an image, how does this image speak to your imagination and what does it open up for you? If it is a symbol, how do you interpret this symbol in the film and in your life? If it is something else, what insights occur?

Responding to the Film

After you have spent time reflecting and being moved by someone or something in the film, listen to your heart. How does your heart want you to respond? What memories from your own life have been triggered by the film? What is the invitation or conversion God is offering you through this film? You might like to respond in an oral or written prayer, or with a gesture or movement.

Resting with God

If you prefer to just rest with what has happened, allow yourself to be silent. Enter into the experience of communion with God. Enter into contemplative prayer. Surrender to just being with whatever has been evoked in you without thoughts, words, feelings, or images.

Closing

Film *divina* has given you an opportunity to hear God speak to your experience of God and life. When you have finished your prayer response, allow God's invitation to be extended into your everyday life. This is a chance to put whatever you have learned into action. Let yourself be playful and creative in your response.

Practical Applications

- Choose a film that you are drawn to. Any film that moves you can be valuable.
- Turn on the film when you feel relaxed and attentive.
- Pay attention to where you connect in a special way with the plot, an image, a character, a line in the film, a conversation between characters, a moment of conversion, or a symbol.
- Replay, in your mind or on the actual TV screen, the portion of the film that speaks to you.
- Attend to whatever captures your attention; see what it evokes in you.
- Let your heart respond in its own way to the conversion God is offering you through this film. Respond in an oral or written prayer, with movement, or with silence.

Example of Film *Divina* through Use of the Movie *Matilda* by *Sr. Mary Giles Mailhot, OSB*

Character I connect with:

In the movie *Matilda* I connected most with the main character. Matilda is a little girl born into the "wrong" family. She loves to learn especially through the many books she brings home from the library. Eventually she finds a kind teacher who encourages her and a magical power within herself.

Scenes I remember well:
- The opening scene is the trip home from the hospital after Matilda's birth. Mom and Dad argue in the front seat while Matilda, in an unsecured baby carrier, slides back and forth behind them. She looks mildly surprised but not scared.
- Matilda as a very young child discovers the adventure in books. She figures out how to go to the library and walks

there by herself. Using her toy wagon, she brings home dozens of books.

- School-aged Matilda becomes very angry and hurt at being mistreated by an exaggeratedly mean principal. She begins to discover her unique power: to make things move by willing it. The kitchen scene, set to music, when she makes various objects dance with her is utterly delightful. She will learn to use her power to help herself and others.

Reflection:

Sometimes I feel like a misfit, an oddball. I become frustrated and angry. I feel misunderstood and judged. Whew! There is a lot of energy around this today. What's the prayer in this? After letting the energy lead me, I hear this question: Where does this energy need to be used? Matilda found her unique gift when she let her anger-energy become creative. Right now, I don't know what my anger might create, so my prayer for now is, "Thank you, God, for this anger-energy. Let it be a reminder of the creative power you've given me. Let my energy be co-creative."

Mantra:

My mantra into silence today is *co-create.* I will breathe in and out with this prayer intention until I can be still in silence with our Creator.

Praying with the Body: *Motio Divina*

Motio divina, or praying with our bodies, may involve simple body movements, such as yoga postures or dance movements. Miriam the prophetess responded to God's redemption of the Israelites with the natural movements of her body. She took up the tambourine and led all the women in song and dance giving praise and thanks to God (Exod 15:21–22). She felt the movement of the Spirit within herself and invited the people to dance with her.

We focus now on how we too can use natural body movements when responding to scripture. You will need to select an excerpt from scripture that draws you. *Motio divina* is an opportunity to use body movements to answer questions: "How does this text speak to me? What embodied prayer response does it elicit from me?"

Preparation

There are several options for you in preparing for *motio divina*. One way is to attend to your breathing. First, become aware of your breath at first without changing its pattern. Just notice the gentle inhalation and exhalation of your body that helps to sustain your life. Offer a prayer of gratitude for this holy and life-giving breath. Gently draw your breath deeper, allowing your chest to expand. See if you can bring your breath all the way into your belly. You may want to place your hands on your belly to feel the rhythm. Then slowly begin to imagine how your breath carries oxygen to your lungs, which release it into your bloodstream to travel throughout your body, bringing nourishment. Visualize your breath filling your lungs and belly and then filling your entire body, moving down through your arms and legs. Bring the attention of your breath to different places in your body and see if you can slowly breathe into those spaces: feet, lower and upper legs, back, shoulders, arms, hands, then your neck and head. With each breath in, receive the life-giving energy. With each breath out, release any tension you may be carrying.

A way to warm up the body is to do a range of movements in the space around you. Begin by standing and being fully present to your body. Step forward slowly and reflect on your intention for this time. Gently step backward and reflect on what has happened in your past and give honor and respect to the experiences that have made you who you are. Step to each side and take a moment to honor the significant relationships in your life and the community that supports you. Raise your hands above your heart and acknowledge your relationship with God the Creator. Place your hands in prayer position in front of your heart to connect to the divine within. Bow slightly to show reverence. Bend down even lower to symbolize your surrender to God.

Another way of warming up the body is to move various parts of the body. Start with the neck and go all the way down. Gently loosen the body's tension by rotating the shoulders, clenching and releasing the fists, shaking the arms and legs. Pay attention to where there might be any tense spots: head, eyes, ears, mouth, nose, neck, spine, chest, breast, arms, fingers, inner organs, genitals, legs, knees, and toes. After you have warmed up your body, lie on the floor. Notice where there are tense places. Invite the tension to melt away. You might imagine the tense area as a pat of butter slowly melting.

Another option for preparation is to play a short piece of rhythmic music. Freely allow yourself to move to the rhythm. Notice where your body feels free and where it is stuck. Be attentive to your body.

Reading, Grounding

Now you are ready to listen to the scripture with your body. Read the passage you have selected and then listen for a word or phrase that invites you to spend time with it. How do these words in the scripture reading speak to you? What feeling does it spark in you? Pay attention to the action that the word or feeling elicits in your body. Move into the posture that expresses the word or feeling going on in you. Let your body bless, delight, desire, groan, weep, hear, lament, long, rest, search; let it be angry, fearful, or joyful. Respond in any way that captures the bodily gesture of your word or feeling. Be grounded in that posture for a few moments and continue to listen to it with your body.

Reflecting, Shaping

Continue to hold your body posture, letting your body's memories speak to you as you make the inner connections. Notice the shape of your body. What does this shape feel like, look like, remind you of, invite you to, call forth in you? What does your body know about the sensation you are experiencing? Listen to your body's wisdom and go wherever it takes you.

Body Prayer

The gesture you have been holding can enhance your prayer. Repeat the gesture as you feel moved to do so. Allow the Spirit to be with you in your prayer. Just as Miriam felt tremendous gratitude and sang and danced her prayer, move with your body in a gesture of blessing, thanksgiving, surrender, awe, wonder, contrition, grief, anger, fear, or whatever expression arises in you. Your posture is your body's dialogue with God. A posture of silence may be the most authentic response for you. Practice trusting your body's messages to you.

Closing

Body prayer opens us to our body wisdom. The body is a place of revelation and says what words cannot. Being in touch with our energy, with *ruah,* which is the breath of God flowing through us, is a sensation defying words. *Motio divina,* our response to scripture, can be prayed in many ways. Be creative and use your imagination in yoga, dance, or song to pray with movement.[12]

Practical Applications

- Attend to your breathing and then warm up your body by doing a range of motions.
- Move various parts of your body, or move with the rhythm of music.
- Choose and read aloud a short portion of scripture.

- Pay attention to the feelings the words stir in you. Express your feelings and thoughts by moving your body.
- Move into the posture that expresses the words or feelings going on in you.
- Continue to hold your body posture; let your body's memories speak to you as you make the inner connections.
- Notice the shape of your body. What does this shape feel like, look like, remind you of, invite you to, call forth in you?
- Use the gesture you have been holding, or a posture of silence, to enhance your prayer.

Example of *Motio Divina* in Doing a Wide Range of Motions
by Julie Barrett Ziegler

I set aside a time, early morning, after the "beginnings" of the day have subsided, and my practical obligations for my family are fulfilled. I remember that doing this deeper work happens more easily for me *before* I have broken my fast (had breakfast). When my body has recently received food, all my physical instincts to digest and create energy take precedent over my intuitive life, so I wait till *after* my morning meditation time to have breakfast. This alone is a discipline toward *lectio*. It is anticipatory, even expectant.

In my prayer space, I give myself enough room to extend my arms, to allow for bending, movement, unencumbered. My clothes are loose, my hair is pulled back, the electric lights are off. I light the nearby candle, and say inwardly, "Here I am, Lord. Good morning. Thank you for another day." On "movement" days, I try to use as few words as possible. I want to invite my *body* to do my talking for me, and hear what God has to say, through the gift of my physical being. I stand, trying to come to stillness, yet very aware of the hard floor beneath my feet, the chill in the early morning air.

Physical sensation takes on more "volume" in my inner hearing as I close my eyes, and begin to lean, gently, from side to side. A thought: How many people do not have the privilege of this morning time? I remember my own frantic mornings when my children were young, and let the thought go, just be in my feet, my knees, my legs...

My simple movements are very closely connected and inspired by my breathing—rhythmic, small, but going deeper, as I begin to bend my knees, to give way to the immense reality of gravity. Could I sink right down through the floor? What lies beneath me, who came before me, what was here before this room, this house, this road? A plié, a ballet movement, a bowing, to the immensity of matter, beneath me, supporting me. Thoughts...questions...I let them move through me as I breathe and begin to sway. I lift myself up with a big intake of breath—raising my hands above me, feeling the stretch of the muscles in my back, my arms...Where are you leading me, Lord? What is ahead, above, beyond this day? I let the thoughts rise up and flow from my fingers out into the air, into the world, into space, into God's big "catcher's mitt."

Now, side to side—my arms lifting like wings, making gentle circles round my middle. Who is with me? Who helps me? Who needs me? Who is too close, too far, too much, not enough? God knows this. Do I? Leaning backward, how far can I bend without losing my balance?...A face, unbidden—my Gramma Marian—always bending so far for her family—how did she keep her balance? Let the thought go—send it out with my hand moving from front to back.

I lean forward—surprising myself that this is more difficult, especially with eyes closed...Is this how I am moving toward my own future? Breathe out, lean back to center, till I stand straight again. My feet are feeling rooted to the floor...my knees wanting to stretch out into walking...no, stay present, stay in this circling, rounding, breathing, yes, stay present, my spirit within this slowly spinning top of physical being...God spins me, I whirl fast, I slow down, sometimes I topple over. God spins me again...breathe.

Now I feel the movement wanting to suspend—I bring my arms around me, still moving side to side more slowly, crossing over my heart, hands at my shoulders, hugging myself—God hugging me, through the gift of this body, this vessel, for experiencing movement, breath. How good it is just to B R E A T H E. Gratitude. Loosening of muscles, emotions...Oh yeah, I remember, memory lives in the muscle tissue of the body...How will I move this body this day, how will I move my spirit in my body this day? I move into *intention,* and leave the question behind me. I will be my best self this day. I will try.

I come to stillness, feel the floor, hear the small, simple noises of the house...I come back. I feel more ready for this day. I feel more present in my body. I bow, in gratitude, to the Unseen Guest, and take a step out of the circle of movement that has given me a new sense of calm. I take a cleansing breath and step into the day.

Conclusion

In this chapter we have explored a wide variety of ways in which journaling and the arts can enhance your experience of praying *lectio divina* and move you into deeper reflection. We have seen many ways to encounter God in "texts" beyond scripture. Honor those forms of prayer that facilitate your deepening relationship with God.

We have also offered practical suggestions for working with various forms of *lectio divina,* as well as offered examples of personal experiences people have had as they sought to listen to God speak through the senses.

CHAPTER TEN

The Transformational
Value of Lectio

[God] will be all that we are zealous for, all that we strive for.
[God] will be all that we think about, all our living,
all that we talk about, our very breath.
—John Cassian, *Conferences* 10:7[1]

In this book we have journeyed deeper and deeper through the various "moments" of *lectio divina*. In this final chapter we summarize the journey we have taken and explore how practicing *lectio divina* regularly can infuse our daily life with an awareness of the sacredness of all things.

Listening to All of Life

We have learned about the various phases of *lectio divina* and explored its history as a treasured practice among those who value God's revelation through sacred texts. We have learned the value of making space in our lives for the gentle whisper of the holy so that it can weave itself into the whole of our lives. We have seen how *lectio divina* increases our awareness of the sacred dimension in our interactions with other people, in our work, and in our leisure time.

Through the practice of listening, we develop a deeper level of awareness. When we commit to a regular practice of prayer, the fruits of prayer begin to weave themselves into the whole of our lives. Through prayer, our awareness of God's presence and love grows and gradually fills our whole being. When prayer spills over into all of life, we approach the world differently. Instead of being satisfied with the surface level of meaning, we look for the deeper dimensions of things we see and experience. We become more conscious of God's presence in all things and are able to more readily receive the gift of that presence in our everyday lives.

We have explored several ways to savor scripture, stay with it, and allow it to permeate our whole being. Scripture can nourish us in ways we can not anticipate. When we savor the Word, we begin to really taste life. When we taste life, our hearts respond and we express our growth in the way we live our lives.

Author Christopher Bamford writes that the desert fathers and mothers read and contemplated the biblical text not to gain knowledge but to enter into a way of life: "*To read was to do. It was to become what one read or contemplated. To understand the Scriptures was to live them*"[2] (emphasis his). The purpose of *lectio divina* was an encounter with God that would lead to a new way of being in the world. The regular practice of *lectio* invites us to look and listen deeply so that we can discover God working in ways we might not see or hear otherwise. As we listen for God's invitation in the text, we grow more deeply aware of what God is demanding of our lives. As our prayer of listening expands to our whole life, we begin to hear God's invitation in the events, situations, and persons around us.

Each morning that we wake up to another day, we have an opportunity to explore the depths of the world and of God's presence pulsing at the heart of it. Every day we give ourselves the gift of time and space for *lectio divina* and contemplative prayer, we practice a way of being that spills over into the world. This gift we give ourselves also becomes a gift to others.

Lectio divina teaches us the discipline of accepting each moment of life as it arrives. We learn to listen in the moment for God's voice speaking to our circumstances. We grow in faith and trust that God is always speaking to us and inviting us forward and deeper into our lives. We discover new ways to be open to God's gifts as we experience our work, our friends, and our home.

We begin to notice how we are growing and we even loosen our controlling grip on life. We not only become present to God, we also become alive to God's presence and celebrate it all around us.

Responding to All of Life

Praying *lectio divina* with scripture is meant to engage the whole of us, body *and* soul. We come to know the scriptures more intimately by studying them and living them through our own life experiences. Prayer slowly becomes woven into all we do. We grow in our awareness of the holiness of all things: "Every creature, like every sacred word, [is a] theophany. The rays of divinity pierce through everywhere."[3] The contemplative is one who sees the holy in all of creation. As we develop a contemplative spirit, we begin to hear God speaking to us through every voice and encounter. Joan Chittister observes:

> The real contemplative hears the voice of God in the voice of the other, sees the face of God in the face of the other, knows the will of God in the person of the other, serves the heart of God by addressing the wounds [and] answering the call of the other.[4]

Prayer becomes less about perfect performance and more about the quality of our everyday lives. Prayer is a unifying force that helps to bring together all the fragments of ourselves into a unified whole. The awareness of God we cultivate through *lectio divina* is slowly integrated into how we live our lives. This is a process of increasing depth: a rhythm of response that permeates every aspect of our lives. We live into a deeper way of life, one sparked by a profound awareness of the sacred. Prayer enables us to stand before the world in awe and receive the many gifts hidden there.

Becoming "Heart People" with "Heart Intelligence"

To be a contemplative it is necessary to take time every day for the practices that lead our hearts to the heart of the divine. In chapter 2 we briefly explored the biblical view of the heart as the very center of each person. It is the place where our will, our desires, and our hopes come together. In the development of the Christian spiritual tradition, the heart center was known as "the place where we are in most intimate contact with God's presence and with our essential union with others, where the deep, ongoing love affair between God and human beings actually takes place."[5] In the monastic tradition, there is a profound recognition that a prayerful life is possible only for those who have made their hearts vulnerable, as they bring their whole hearts to God. We are called to examine the places where our hearts feel divided and to bring our hearts to God in prayer so that they can be made whole again.

Saint Benedict, who was filled with biblical understanding, uses the word *heart* thirty-one times in his *Rule*.[6] His Prologue begins by inviting us to listen with the ear of our heart. For Benedict, listening to all of life in this way, with our whole being, is how we hear and respond to God. It comes from the very center of our being and is a very intimate form of listening.

Benedict emphasizes the importance of preparing our hearts and bodies so we can be a continuous listening presence before God. Daily preparation is needed: "Every day the contemplative makes a new beginning, tries again to plumb the meaning of life, disappears again into the heart of God so present in the world around us if we only realize it."[7] We are invited to live with a heart that yearns for life, a heart that desires God, and a heart that delights in the voice of God. The invitation is always there even if it is difficult for us to respond. In the *Rule*, we hear God reassuring us from the scriptures: "Once you have done this, my eyes will be upon you and my ears will listen for your prayers; and even before you ask me, I will say to you: Here I am" (*RB* Prologue 18).

Throughout the *Rule,* St. Benedict discusses how the heart helps shape our way of life. We are invited to love God with our whole heart (*RB* 4.1). Sometimes our hearts are divided or they resist God. Then we follow only our own desires without attending to what God desires for us (*RB* 3.8). God searches our minds and hearts to see how well we love in our daily lives (*RB* 7.14). We grow by being mindful of our thoughts and the feelings of our hearts. When we recognize how destructive some thoughts are, we can give them to the Merciful One and receive a blessing. The heart is able to expand in its capacity to receive and give God's love. As we recognize God's tremendous love for us, we grow in our love for others. This is a progressive journey, one that takes a lifetime to unfold.

The contemplative journey usually begins with an experience of compunction. The word *compunction* comes from the Latin *compunctio,* meaning a sting or prick of the conscience. Compunction of the heart essentially means we have been stung by the truth: it has shaken us out of our complacency and moved us toward action. When our conscience has been touched, we are freed from self-delusion and deception. This is the dynamic nature of conversion and how the heart changes. We are shocked by the truth of something we had not seen before. The pain that comes with this realization is also liberating; it frees us from our unhealthy assumptions. It is transforming because it renews our desire for God. We have a clearer vision of what it is God is calling us to. We begin to change our lives to reflect what God desires for our lives. Out of this experience flows a single-minded attention on God: the Latin phrase "*intentio cordis* refers to the single outward movement of the heart in the direction of God which becomes possible when outward clamor recedes."[8] *Lectio divina* can affect this slow conversion of the heart. It can help us shed old attitudes to make way for new ones. Purity of heart is the result of a contemplative attitude which seeks to live a simplified, integrated, and harmonious life of interior freedom. The contemplative heart is not divided but operates out of a desire to be one with God.

The lifelong process of awakening to truth, and the conversion of the heart to God's desires for us, lead to the expansion of our hearts. We can no longer limit our love simply to ourselves and those closest to us, but we grow in love for others and for all of creation. As we walk the contemplative path, "our hearts will overflow with the inexpressible delight of love" (*RB* Prologue 49).

Grateful Living and *Lectio*

When we live out of an awareness of our union with God and others, we live a life full of gratitude. Gratitude is a natural response to God's abundant gifts. Our gratitude deepens as we develop an "appreciative eye." Jacqueline Kelm, in her book *Appreciative Living: The Principles of Appreciative Inquiry in Personal Life,* speaks of appreciating the present, imaging what we want more of, and striving to live an aligned, integrated life. Living in an appreciative, contemplative way opens us up to receive wisdom and enlightenment about what is best for us and for others. Because *lectio divina* reminds us of God's never-ending invitation to live life fully, we put energy into living in a positive mode, which magnifies positive possibilities. We notice what creates richer life experiences and we increasingly embody our deepest desires.[9]

Scripture emphasizes the importance of gratitude and shows us the way to *live* our thankfulness. Scripture is a source of guidance and wisdom for us. When we immerse ourselves in sacred texts through *lectio divina,* we are developing a greater ability to see what we want more of in life. Reflection time enables us to be more in tune with God's invitation of how to live more fully. A contemplative vision allows us to glimpse what is possible and through this awareness to create more of what God wants for us in life.

An unconditionally positive attitude moves us toward more positive experiences in life. Positive images help us to see new possibilities and to eventually create a transformed world. A positive attitude not only impacts our experience of life, it also influences the emotions of others as well. Daniel Goleman theorizes about social intelligence in his book *Social Intelligence.* Stephen Kiesling quotes Goleman's ideas on the neuroscience of relationships:

These mirror neurons are part of a neural network called the social brain, which is designed to connect us to the person we're with in a very intimate way—a brain-to-brain bridge that puts us on the same wavelength, not just metaphorically, but actually, so that our brain construct is a representation of what's going on inside the other person and melds our moods and emotions. This goes on constantly in every interaction, whether we know it or not. So if you are with someone angry, it will create an echo in you, whether or not the person is angry with you. The same is true of joy and happiness.[10]

Whatever we are feeling has an impact on the feelings of others. The practice of *lectio divina* not only changes our lives, it also influences the lives of others. Scripture challenges us to focus on positive emotions and actions such as hope and strengthens us to live out of our inner core. As we mature in *lectio divina,* others will experience peace, calm, and stability coming from our mirror neurons.

Positive images and emotions lead to positive behaviors. In the scriptures, God blesses us with many kinds of images, especially nurturing ones. Nurturing images expand our power to love. As we are fed in love, we can feed others. The scriptures remind us to move beyond words to actions: "And whatever you do, in word or deed, do everything in the name of the Lord Jesus, giving thanks to God the Father through him" (Col 3:17). The gift of *lectio divina* is that it enables us to integrate our interior and exterior behavior so that we are whole and our actions flow from an attitude of appreciation and love.

Holy Leisure

The contemplative life teaches us the practice of holy leisure. In our Western culture, we are losing our leisure time as we work harder and longer. We are encouraged to fill our time with busyness and productivity. Contemplation invites us to remember that *being* comes before *doing*; it shows us that the quality of our *doing* for God is tied to the quality of our *being* with God. There is tremendous value in making time and space for holy things, those things that make "the human more human by engaging the heart and broadening the vision and deepening the insight and stretching the soul."[11] Holy leisure means stepping back from our busy lives and reflecting on the meaning behind our actions. We are invited to look at our lives through the lens of God's Word.

Through regular contemplative practice and time spent with scripture, we cultivate our capacity for holy leisure and out of that place we are able to ask ourselves, "What is it to follow the gospel in this situation, now, here?....[We take time to wonder] what the Jesus-life demands in this situation."[12]

Final Moment: Action

As the Word of God shapes us and forms who we are, our very being is shared with other people. The Word shapes our experience of every person, event, and action. We become reflections of God's Word and expressions of God's hand in our lives. The fruit of the practice of *lectio divina* is assimilating the Word of God and being assimilated by it. It is a movement from conversation to communion.

As we have already seen, the steps of *lectio divina* are often referred to by their Latin names: *lectio, meditatio, oratio,* and *contemplatio.* There is an additional step, mentioned earlier, sometimes called *operatio,* or action, which is the moment when we end our prayer and return to daily life. This step includes all of our time until we next sit down again to *lectio divina. Operatio* is about taking our prayer into our everyday lives and responding to our lives as a constant prayer. The act of praying *lectio divina* makes a difference in our inner world that extends to the outer world: God asks us to consider what actions in our lives will expand our hearts and bring greater compassion to others. Entering into a deeper relationship with God through *lectio div-*

ina makes demands on our lives: "God invites us to act and then empowers us, directing our steps in the way of peace."[13] The contemplative expands his or her gaze from the scripture to the whole world, to see things through the eyes of God and to live out the ways of God.

Through regular prayer and the practice of *lectio divina,* we slowly come to realize our dependence on God and the dependence of all things on God. This awareness gives us "a sense of interdependence with all God's people and at the same time the responsibility we have toward them. True contemplation inevitably creates a social consciousness."[14] There are many actions that express loving-kindness to the world around us. It is especially important for kindness to be prompted by an awareness of the ways in which the freedom of others has been limited by poverty, war, racism, and other acts of oppression. Once we become aware of these injustices, our connection with the God of love and life moves us beyond ourselves and leads us to express our love in tangible ways in the world. Just as God works in us as we pray through the steps of *lectio divina,* so grace supports and guides us in our loving action in the world.

Lectio Divina with Life Experience

In chapter 9 we offered some possible ways of using *lectio divina* to pray with a variety of sacred texts including poetry, visual art, and music. Another sacred text we might consider praying with is our life experience. Each moment of our lives is ripe with meaning and possibility yet we often only see this when we take time to reflect. We invite you to consider expanding your *lectio divina* practice by focusing on your daily life experience as a sacred text. It is yet another way to be attentive to the ways God is working. When we experience our lives as vessels of holiness, we come to appreciate how God delights in us and the gifts we offer to the world.

Preparation

Prepare for your prayer time as you normally do by using whatever method helps you open to God. Allow yourself to rest in silence for a few moments. Become as fully present to God as you can in this moment, adopt a posture of deep listening, and be ready to receive the gifts hidden in your daily life.

Listening for God's Word in Your Life (Lectio)

Move into *lectio* by taking time to recall a specific experience you would like to pray with. You might instead want to reflect on the whole day that has passed. In your imagination, reenter this particular time and place or walk through your day again. Move around and explore; notice the conversations, the colors and images, the feelings you experienced. Notice the times when you felt especially moved by something: joy, sadness, or anger. As you move through these moments, pay attention to what you see, hear, smell, taste, and touch. Notice where you experienced the most intense energy and where those energy levels shifted. Savor each moment and gather them into your depths. Listen for a word, a phrase, a symbol, a feeling, or a particular moment that captures your attention. Watch for the thing that shimmers; look for what beckons you, invites you, or addresses you. There may be a moment that unnerves you, disturbs you, or stirs you. Listen for the moment in your experience that seems especially ripe with meaning and then revisit it in your imagination. Take time to savor it.

Reflecting on God's Word in Your Life (Meditatio)

Reflect on your experience again and continue to savor the moment that draws you. Allow the word or phrase, the image, or the feeling to unfold in your memory and imagination and to work within you. Let it speak even more deeply. Notice what other feelings or images arise for you. Allow the Spirit to expand your capacity for listening and to open you to a fuller experience of this moment. What do you see, hear, touch, or feel? Allow this experience to interact with your thoughts, hopes, memories, and desires. Rest in this awareness for some time.

Responding to God's Word in Your Life (Oratio)

After a time of resting in this experience you will be moved to deeper insight and a desire to respond and say yes to God. When this time comes, enter into the experience again and attend to the way this moment unfolds and connects with the situation in your life right now. Ask yourself how it relates to what you heard and saw during the day. How does it connect with what is happening at home, work, or leisure? Take an extended time to explore this connection. Look for the ways God is present to you. Is God calling you to anything new in your present circumstances? Is there a challenge being presented? Address your response to God in whatever way seems appropriate. Allow your whole being to become a prayer by honestly expressing your deepest thoughts, feelings, and desires to God. Open yourself to being touched and changed by the Word of God. Rest in this prayer for some time.

Resting with God's Word in Your Life (Contemplatio)

Finally, simply rest in the presence of the One who has spoken to you intimately and personally. Allow yourself to simply *be* in God's presence. Practice silence and let go of your own words. Practice receptivity and take in all that God offers in this moment. Rest in the silence of God's loving embrace and allow your heart to be moved to gratitude for this time of prayer. Rest in this loving space as long as you need.

Closing

Take a few moments to reflect on how this prayer felt for you. How did your life experience speak to you as a sacred text? Were you able to hear God's voice? Let the moment that captured your attention linger with you throughout the day and be open to new insights God might give you.

Conclusion: Becoming Fire

The following story contains a wonderful image of how we can become fire through our *lectio divina* experiences:

> Abba Lot went to see Abba Joseph and said to him, "Abba, as far as I can I say my little office, I fast a little, I pray and meditate, I live in peace and as far as I can, I purify my thoughts. What else can I do?" Then the old man stood up and stretched his hands towards heaven. His fingers became like ten lamps of fire and he said to him, "If you will, you can become all flame."[15]

This story invites us to listen for God, first in the scriptures, and then to slowly expand our loving gaze to the whole world. Then we are invited to "become fire." What does this mean for you? When prayer and attending to the sacred have become so deeply integrated into your life that you are consumed by a love of God and all things, you have become fire. The practice of *lectio divina* opens us up to this experience of God. Faithfulness in prayer creates a burning flame within you that wants to burst forth into the world and express the wonderful things you have seen and heard. When your heart is filled with gratitude at the beauty of the world and God's gifts, you have become fire. Fire is, of course, one of the images for the Holy Spirit. At Pentecost, the apostles are gathered together in fear about what would happen after Jesus' death. Divine fire descends on them and empowers them:

Its power touches them at the very core of their being, and frees the Word....to take on a multiplicity of forms, each of them rendered profoundly personal and at the same time universal....The Word of fire will pour forth, in an ever more universal way, because it will flow out of hearts profoundly sensitive to its action, hearts penetrated by it, unified by it, joined by it.[16]

When we are given the gift of fire, our souls become illuminated and we come to live into this fiery presence with our whole being. We are called to tend the fire of our hearts and become a fire of love in the world. We are invited to recognize God, who dwells deeply within each of us as a holy flame. When St. Benedict reached the end of his life, he had a final contemplative vision of the whole world in a single ray of burning light.[17] Hopefully this book has inspired you to grow in your life of prayer by spending time in the practice of *lectio divina* and to experience the "burning light" of God's love in and through you. May your prayers become a fire within you to light your way.

Practical Applications for Praying with Today

- How have I discovered God working in ways today I did not expect?
- What is God's invitation to me in the circumstances of my life today?
- Where have I experienced God's voice, face, desire, will, or heart today?
- How have I experienced the sacred today?
- How have I yearned for life and desired God in each moment of my life today?
- How did I experience compunction or reframe a truth today?
- What new insight was I given today?

- How have I lived a simplified, integrated, harmonious life today?
- How did my "appreciative eye" see more today? How did I live in alignment with that new vision?
- What new possibility in my life did I catch a glimpse of today?
- What meaning do I find behind my actions of today?
- How did I follow the Gospel in the here and the now of today?
- What actions in my life helped expand my heart and brought greater compassion to others today?

Practical Applications for Praying with Life Experiences

- Rest in silence for a few moments.
- Take time to recall a specific experience you want to pray or reflect on.
- Remember the conversations, the colors and images, the feelings, what you saw, heard, smelled, tasted, or touched.
- Remember where you experienced the most intense energy.
- Listen for a word, a phrase, a symbol, a feeling, or a particular moment that captured your attention. Repeat it; savor it in your imagination.
- Reflect on your experience and continue to savor the moment. Allow the Spirit to expand your capacity for listening and to open you to a fuller experience of this moment.
- Allow it to interact with your thoughts, memories, and desires.
- Attend to the way the unfolding of the moment connects with the context and situation of your life right now. How is God present there? Is God calling you to anything new in your present circumstances?
- Address your response to God in whatever way seems appropriate.
- Allow your whole being to become prayer by honestly expressing your deepest thoughts, feelings, and desires to God.

- Open yourself to be touched and changed by the Word of God.
- Rest in the presence of God's loving embrace and allow your heart to be moved to gratitude for this time of prayer.

An Example of a Personal Reflection on *Lectio Divina* with a Life Experience *by a Retreatant*

A participant in a retreat entitled "*Lectio Divina* on Life: Healing for the Spirit" wrote about her experience of using *lectio* in her life and with her illness:

Using scripture in the method of *lectio* for prayer has been a part of my life for some forty years as a member of a religious community. It helps me so much to take the line or two that *jump* out at me from the daily scripture readings and pray over it all day. I like to see where God leads me with it throughout the day. Often it helps me to have the experience that God is with me or...how God might bring me to an awareness of what's happening in the moment with another person or...some surprising take on how I've been acting at the time. Sometimes something in my day will bring it back to my mind or heart. I often lean on its strength and good advice...like God's voice encouraging me, blessing me, challenging me. Some of those lines of scripture have become lines that recur in my prayer. For me, it is often when those lines of scripture are put to music that I remember them best.

At times, the lines from scripture or from the life experiences of those I minister to...bless, encourage, and often challenge and stretch me in my own life. I feel invited to look at my own life differently. But nothing touched me more, stretched me, offered big changes and challenges, and helped me bond and be at one with others in their lives and prayer than my experiences of being ill, which began in January 2003.

In January 2003, I spent three weeks in Asia with sisters of my religious community as part of my sabbatical time. After I flew back to the United States, I felt very tired, like I had an infection. The tests my doctor took showed the surprising results of a large hard tumor in my left kidney. What a shock and what a switch in "my" plans and what I thought God was leading me to as well. I had my left kidney removed on May 8, 2003. The next month or so was full of experiences of pain and recovery woes...lots of fatigue and bouts of nausea and vomiting as I couldn't seem to find a pain medication that didn't react negatively on me. Prayer was one of dryness and not much focusing. I often held my rosary, tried to image my hand in the hand of Jesus, and just said, "Help me, God!"

Because the cancer was contained within my left kidney and had not spread, I didn't need chemotherapy or radiation, just frequent checkups for some time. This should have felt like the great news it was. However, my spirits were still dragging. I kept wondering why I had retinal problems and now kidney cancer. Had I done or not done something to cause them? What should I be doing to keep cancer and retinal problems at bay? What was God trying to tell me?

Seven months after my surgery, when I finally felt well enough, I made an eight-day retreat to ask God to help me explore what the kidney cancer might mean to my spirit. People had suggested to me how I had worked too hard and too long, how I hadn't taken time off, how I hadn't taken care of my stress, and how cancer was in my family history as "reasons" for my cancer. Sometimes, these people felt like Job's friends to me. My spiritual director urged me to bring these questions to prayer, as well as to use my kidney as the text for *lectio divina* meditation and journaling. She hoped this might help me explore and symbolize what I'd been experiencing and to see with "new eyes" where God was inviting me to grow and to find meaning in it all.

My spiritual director also suggested that I pray with Psalm 16:7, which reads, "In the night also my *heart* instructs me." She also shared a Benedictine scholar's recent finding from her Hebrew Scripture studies. The Hebrews, she said, used *kidneys* as another word for *heart* (or the center of a person's emotions and conscience). I laughed as I prayed the first time with this line. At this time in my life, I do get up at night with my "kidneys." Some other lines from Ezekiel 36:25–27 came to me. They read: "From all your idols I will cleanse you. A new heart I will give you, and a new spirit I will put within you; and I will remove from your body the heart of stone and give you a heart of flesh. I will put my spirit within you."

I prayed then about my kidney, which had had a big stony heart in it, and pondered what was "stony" in me that God wanted to take out and replace with a new heart. God invited me to see with new eyes and listen with a new heart to what God was awakening me to. I knew I needed God to draw very close to help me lean into the pain of it so I could "see."

One thing that came to me was that God wanted to heal a resentment that had hardened within me concerning another sister. God awakened me to and invited me to take responsibility to acknowledge my anger and to forgive and reconcile with this sister. God showed me this so gently. I knew that the grace of God's forgiveness was already within me. I had only to be aware of it, choose it, and act upon it.

I heard God telling me in my prayer that I was to give up guilt or shame about my "hard heart" as well. Part of the new heart God gave me was a heart to forgive and love myself. With this gift, I could forgive and love others for the unique selves that they are. I could also face my own complicity in maintaining distance from this sister. I was invited to treasure her otherness as gift, rather than figure her out or remold her to someone who looked more like me.

My cancer brought me up short and asked me, "Why have you waited?...Why are you waiting?" With God's grace, I am changing and living into the healing, forgiveness, and reconciliation necessary to reach out and connect with those who appear "other" or "different." Instead of being bent over with the "otherness" of my cancer or of my sister's challenge, God is helping me stand up and love in a new way with this gift. Somehow, God is showing me, in being different from another, what is unique and valuable about both of us...which I may not have known outside my relationship with them. I can risk more often "seeing" God coming to me in honesty and rebuke as well as in the encouragement of others. I hear God inviting me to use the stone that has been in my heart as a steppingstone to a new way of relating to myself and others, not something that weighs my heart down.

My scar and the initial emptiness of and pain in the space where my kidney had been remind me that God reached out and will continue to reach out to refresh my heart. After being such a do-er in my life, I was being asked to turn control over to the Spirit's guidance. Like Jacob who wrestled with a stranger all night and was left limp, I am also marked for life with this experience and others that continue to come along at my age. Along with Jacob, I know the grace of disruption. I ask for the blessing God wants to give me through these challenges. I pray to slow down and to surrender to this new rhythm of redeeming grace. I trust it is already happening in me.

My cancer gave me a new experience of membership and community. It led me to a bond of communion with those who suffer "brokenness" in any way....I know sorrow and even joy at a joining of my life with theirs. I know in a different way that experiences of impasse and paralysis that illness brings also hold potential for creativity in my response to them....With Julian of Norwich, I pray "to behold God in everything,"[18] to keep choosing the joy, hope, love, and mercy that God offers me, and to be a mirror of this transcendent gift to others in my life and ministry.

A Chapter-by-Chapter Summary of Ways to Practice Lectio Divina

Chapter 1. What Is Lectio Divina?

- Select a regular place for daily *lectio* that is free from distractions.
- Create a prayer space for *lectio*.
- Choose a short scripture passage, preferably from the Gospels, daily readings of the church, or the psalms.

Chapter 2. Deep Listening

- Dedicate a specific time for *lectio* that will work best for you in your daily schedule. Begin with a brief period and try to increase that to twenty or thirty minutes.
- Close your eyes. Relax your body part by part by being aware of your body sensations. Keep moving your attention every few seconds to different parts of your body, especially the places that are tense.
- Notice your breathing. As you breathe in, be aware of the presence of the Spirit filling you; as you breathe out, let go of all that distracts you from this time of prayer.
- Listen with new ears and see with new eyes, with a spirit of openness to the unexpected. Listen and look with love.
- Set aside expectations and assumptions if you can.
- Open your hands to receive.

- Maintain a good posture.
- Move into *lectio* when you feel fully present and ready to listen to God's voice.

Chapter 3. Reading for Formation

- Read the text aloud at least once and then repeat it more slowly until you are stopped by a word or phrase that speaks to your heart.
- Practice surrendering to the moment.
- Embrace what emerges and trust what is revealed.
- Give yourself permission to receive whatever happens.
- Repeat the word or phrase to yourself, savor it, and relish the sound and sense.
- Bring your life experience to prayer.

Chapter 4. Savoring the Word

- Stop reading and begin to meditate when your heart is touched.
- Create a space for the word or phrase. Reflect on it. Repeat it. Memorize it.
- Chew the word or phrase slowly and savor it.
- Slow down, taste, linger, and enjoy the word or phrase.
- Repeat the word or phrase often with your mind and voice.
- Allow the words to stir images, feelings, and memories.
- Be open to the way the word or phrase is working in your heart.
- Notice what is emerging.
- Allow the senses to evoke images and reveal new meanings.
- Listen to how your body responds.
- Tend to the longings awakened by the Word of God within.
- Allow the Word of God to awaken your imagination.
- Repeat the word or phrase throughout the day; allow *lectio divina* to overflow into daily life.

Chapter 5. Responding to a Touched Heart

- Recognize that prayer is the response sparked in us when our hearts have first been touched.
- Stay with the words you have meditated on and then respond from the deepest part of you.
- Pay attention to the emotions evoked.
- Savor the word or phrase and respond out of that experience.
- Discover the mutual longing between you and God.
- Ask yourself, "What is God's invitation to me today?"
- Respond in prayer.
- Be open to saying yes to God's work within us.
- Let *lectio* overflow into your day so that your life becomes a prayer.

Chapter 6. Contemplative Awakening and Awareness

- Release all words, images, or thoughts.
- Be open to God's gift of contemplation by just being in silence.
- Select a one- or two-syllable word or image that is a symbol of your intention to consent to God's presence or action within.
- Sit comfortably with your eyes closed, resting in God.
- Be fully present to God.
- Draw your attention gently back to your surroundings at the end of your prayer practice.
- End the practice period with a gentle recitation of the Lord's Prayer or a psalm.

Chapter 7. Lectio as Scripture Study, Prayer, and Living

- Read aloud slowly a small portion of Psalm 8 (orientation), or Psalm 13 (disorientation), or Psalm 30 (new orientation).

- Notice the word, phrase, or image where God invites you to stop.
- Spend time savoring that word, phrase, or image.
- Notice if an emotion is stirred in you.
- Reflect on how the word, phrase, or emotion leads you to
   √ *Orientation:* Life is stable, balanced, safe, and orderly; God is faithful, stable, and good;
   √ *Disorientation:* Life is chaotic, dark, and painful; God is absent or hidden, or;
   √ *New orientation:* Life is dark, you are barely hanging on, and then God surprises you with new life; God responds to your lament, and you celebrate this new awareness with praise.
- Let your reflection lead you to respond to God and life.
- Pray in response to what stirred in you.

Chapter 8. Shortened Lectio for Busy Days

Beginning the Day

- Pray: "Spirit, help me to be present to you."
- Read the scripture verse or verses aloud slowly several times.
- Use all your senses: speak, hear, taste, savor, smell, and feel the words.
- Pay attention to the word, phrase, image, or feeling that speaks to your heart and invites you to linger.
- Savor, chew, and digest what you have read.
- Linger with a word, phrase, feeling, image, or insight that speaks to your heart.
- Tend it. Pay attention to it.
- Assimilate it. Let it become a part of you. Relish it.
- Memorize whatever speaks to your heart.
- Carry the words into your day either by memorizing them, writing them on a card, or posting them in a place where you'll see them often, like your computer screen.
- Listen for God's invitation and put it into action during the day.

During the Day

- Say aloud or think about the word, phrase, image, or feeling that spoke to your heart in your *lectio divina* time.
- Inhale and exhale a breath-prayer.
- Remember that God's presence is always with you.
- Act on your *lectio divina.*
- Invite God to care for you and extend this caring to anyone who comes into your presence.
- Listen to how God's Word speaks to you through persons, events, or circumstances.
- Respond to the movements of your heart.

Concluding the Day

- Repeat the word, phrase, feeling, or image aloud during the day.
- Reflect on how *lectio divina* befriended you today:
  √ How did the wisdom of *lectio* extend to persons, events, or circumstances?
  √ How did *lectio* help you stay connected with God and others?
  √ How did *lectio* expand and fuel your heart?
- Spend a short amount of time praying with your *lectio divina* experience.
- Dialogue with God about what *lectio divina* revealed to you this day.
- Speak to God spontaneously in gratitude, petition, thanksgiving, joy, grief, anger, fear, compassion, or any feeling that is within you.
- Choose to record the scripture verse, phrase, word, image, feeling, reflection, or prayer in your journal.
- Write or draw your prayer.
- Rest in God's presence in silence without any words, images, feelings, or sensations. Just be in communion with God.
- Hold the experience in your memory.

Chapter 9. Journaling, Making Art, and Praying with Art with Lectio

Lectio Divina with a Journal

Journaling Before Lectio Divina

- What is weighing on me or distracting me?

Journaling While Praying Lectio Divina

- Keep your pen on your lap and make notes of what is stirring you. Look at the section in this chapter entitled "Some Ways of Keeping a *Lectio Divina* Journal."
- Record your word or phrase and any reflections you have.
- Write about what energized you during meditation.
- Write your prayer.

Journaling After Lectio Divina

- Record the invitation you received from God during prayer and how you acted upon it.

Lectio Divina and Art-Making

- Explore creative expression with paint, markers, collage, icons, poetry, movement, words, or sound.
- Follow your longings and see where they take your prayer.
- Look at other suggestions given in chapter 9 in the section "Responding to *Lectio Divina* with Art-Making."

Lectio Divina with Poetry

- Prepare yourself by sitting in a comfortable and relaxing position.
- Choose a poem.

- Read it aloud twice.
- Savor each phrase and gather the words into your depths.
- Listen for a word or phrase that captures your attention.
- Read the poem again and let the word or phrase unfold in your memory and imagination.
  √ What do you see, hear, touch, or remember?
  √ What is evoked in you?
  √ Where does this passage touch your life?
- Allow your whole being to respond in a prayerful dialogue.
- Allow yourself to simply *be* in the silence of God's presence without words, thoughts, or images.

Lectio Divina with Icons and Images

- Settle into stillness.
- Gaze upon the image.
- Explore the entire image with your eyes.
- Notice the various colors and shapes, the different figures and symbols.
- Focus slowly on anything in the image that captures your attention.
- Reflect on the part of the icon that captured your attention.
- Let it draw you more deeply into the experience.
- Invite it to unfold in your imagination and notice if it evokes any memories, feelings, or other images.
- Turn your focus to the ways you feel moved to respond.
  √ What is the invitation behind the images, memories, and feelings that unfolded for you?
  √ How is God speaking to your life through this icon?
- Release all the words and images that have been flooding your heart. Simply rest and be.

Lectio Divina with Music

- Choose a piece of music without words. Select a section of the piece, anything from a musical phrase to an entire movement.
- Find a quiet area and settle into silence.

- Listen to the section twice.
  √ Notice the sounds of the notes and silences between them.
  √ Be present to how the music rises and falls in your body and imagination.
  √ Become aware of any dominant sound, image, or feeling that is calling to you.
- Listen to the section again.
  √ Hold the sound, image, or feeling that first called to you.
  √ Let it draw you more deeply into the experience.
  √ Allow it to unfold in your imagination and notice if any memories, feelings, images, or other melodies are evoked.
- Listen to the section again.
  √ How does your heart want to respond?
  √ What invitation is present for you today in the unfolding of sounds, images, memories, and feelings?
  √ How is God speaking to your life in this moment, through this music?
- Spend some time resting in silence and releasing the sounds, feelings, and images that are stirring inside.

Lectio Divina with Movement: *Motio Divina*

- Attend to your breathing and then warm up your body by doing a range of motions.
- Move various parts of your body, or move with the rhythm of music.
- Choose and read a short portion of scripture aloud. Pay attention to the feelings the words stir in you.
- Express your feelings and thoughts by moving your body.
- Move into the posture that expresses the words or feelings going on in you.
- Continue to hold your body posture.
- Let your body's memories speak to you as you make the inner connections.
- Notice the shape of your body. What does this shape feel like, look like, remind you of, invite you to, call forth in you?

- Be aware that the gesture you have been holding can enhance your prayer as can a posture of silence.

Lectio Divina with Movies: Film Divina

- Choose a film that you are drawn to. Any film that moves you can be valuable.
- Turn on the film when you feel relaxed and attentive.
- Pay attention to where you connect in a special way with the plot, an image, a character, a line in the film, a conversation between characters, a moment of conversion, or a symbol.
- Replay a portion of the film, in your mind or on the TV screen, the portion that speaks to you.
- Attend to whatever captures your attention; see what it evokes in you.
- Be open to the ways your heart wants to respond to the conversion God is offering you through this film. Respond in an oral or written prayer, with movement, or in silence.

Chapter 10. The Transformational Value of Lectio

Lectio Divina and Praying with Today

- How have I discovered God working in ways today I did not expect?
- What is God's invitation to me in the circumstances of my life today?
- Where have I experienced God's voice, face, desire, will, or heart today?
- How have I experienced the sacred today?
- How have I yearned for life and desired God in each moment of my life today?
- How did I experience compunction or reframe a truth today?
- What new insight was I given today?
- How have I lived a simplified, integrated, harmonious life today?

- How did my "appreciative eye" see more today? How did I live in alignment with that new vision?
- What new possibility in my life did I catch a glimpse of today?
- What meaning do I find behind my actions of today?
- How did I follow the Gospel in the here and the now of today?
- What actions in my life helped expand my heart and brought greater compassion to others today?

Lectio Divina and Praying with Life Experiences

- Rest in silence for a few moments.
- Take time to recall a specific experience you want to pray or reflect on.
- Notice the conversations, the colors and images, the feelings, what you saw, heard, smelled, tasted, or touched.
- Notice where you experienced the most intense energy.
- Listen for a word, a phrase, a symbol, a feeling, or a particular moment that captured your attention. Repeat it; savor it in your imagination.
- Reflect on your experience and continue to savor the moment. Allow the Spirit to expand your capacity for listening and to open you to a fuller experience of this moment.
- Allow it to interact with your thoughts, memories, and desires.
- Attend to the way the unfolding of the moment connects with the context and situation of your life right now. How is God present there? Is God calling you to anything new in your present circumstances?
- Address your response to God in whatever way seems appropriate.
- Allow your whole being to become prayer by honestly expressing your deepest thoughts, feelings, and desires to God.
- Open yourself to be touched and changed by the Word of God.
- Rest in the presence of God's loving embrace and allow your heart to be moved to gratitude for this time of prayer.

Notes

Chapter 1. What Is Lectio Divina?

1. Dolores Dowling, "*Lectio*, Our Daily Nourishment for Discernment," *Benedictines* (1996): 10.

2. Ibid., 10.

3. St. Pachomius, *Pachomian Koinonia*, vol. 2, trans. Armand Veilleux (Kalamazoo, MI: Cistercian Publications, 1981), 166.

4. Guigo II, *The Ladder of Monks and Twelve Meditations*, trans. Edmund Colledge and James Walsh (Kalamazoo, MI: Cistercian Publications, 1979), 67–68.

5. Michael Casey, "Saint Benedict's Approach to Prayer," *Cistercian Studies* 15 (1980): 338. Casey considers *humilitas cordis* ("humility of heart"), *puritas cordis* ("purity of heart"), *compunctio cordis* ("compunction of heart"), and *intentio cordis* ("intention of the heart") as essential qualities for Prayer of the Heart. These qualities will be developed in chapter 9, "The Transformational Value of *Lectio*."

Chapter 2. Deep Listening

1. Elisa Davy Pearmain, *Doorways to the Soul: 52 Wisdom Tales from Around the World* (Cleveland, OH: Pilgrim Press, 1998), 14.

2. Michael Casey, *A Guide to Living in the Truth: Saint Benedict's Teaching on Humility* (Liguori, MO: Liguori Publications, 2001), 17.

3. James Martin, *Becoming Who You Are: Insights on the True Self from Merton and Other Saints* (Mahwah, NJ: Paulist Press, 2006).

Chapter 3. Reading for Formation

1. John Cassian, *Conferences,* trans. Colm Luibeid, Classics of Western Spirituality Series (New York: Paulist Press, 1985), 164.

2. Guigo II, *The Ladder of Monks,* trans. Edmund Colledge and James Walsh (Kalamazoo, MI: Cistercian Publications, 1979), 67–68.

3. Ambrose Wathen, "Monastic *Lectio:* Some Clues from Terminology," *Monastic Studies* 12 (1976): 209. Wathen bases his ideas on Forcellini's *Lexicon Totius Latinitatis III* (Padua, 1940), 49–50 and 54–55 as cited in his article.

4. Timothy Fry, ed., *RB 1980* (Collegeville, MN: The Liturgical Press, 1981), 551. *Vacare* is used in *RB* 48:4, 10, 13, 14, 17, 18, 22, and 23.

5. Macrina Wiederkehr, *A Tree Full of Angels: Seeing the Holy in the Ordinary* (San Francisco: HarperSanFrancisco, 1990), 53.

6. Jean Leclercq, *The Love of Learning and the Desire for God: A Study of Monastic Culture* (New York: Fordham University Press, 1982), 15.

7. Michael Casey, *Sacred Reading: The Ancient Art of Lectio Divina* (Liguori, MO: Liguori Publications, 1996), 103.

8. Ibid., 63–70. Casey develops the literal sense in chapter 3 of his book under the topic of "Levels of Meaning."

9. David Noel Freedman, Gary A. Herion, and John David Pleins, eds., *The Anchor Bible Dictionary,* vol. 3 H–J (New York: Doubleday, 1992), 292–93.

10. Ibid., 295.

11. William R. Farmer, ed., *The International Bible Commentary* (Collegeville, MN: The Liturgical Press, 1998), 1116.

Chapter 4. Savoring the Word

1. Marie-Francois Herbaux, "Formation in *Lectio Divina,*" *Cistercian Studies* 18 (1982): 132. The quote is taken from St. Jerome, Letter CXXV, 7.11 to the monk Rusticus, PL 22.

2. Dolores Dowling, "*Lectio,* Our Daily Nourishment for Discernment," *Benedictines* (1996): 12.

3. Fred Bryant, *Savoring: A New Model of Positive Experience* (Mahwah, NJ: Lawrence Erlbaum Associates, 2006), 8–9.

4. Ibid., 138–39.

5. Dowling, 12. Originally this quote was taken from Andrew Louf, *Teach Us to Pray* (Chicago: Franciscan Herald Press, 1975).

6. Macrina Wiederkehr, *A Tree Full of Angels: Seeing the Holy in the Ordinary* (San Francisco: HarperSanFrancisco, 1990), 54.

7. Jean Leclercq, *The Love of Learning and the Desire for God* (New York: Fordham University Press, 1982), 75–76.

Chapter 5. Responding to a Touched Heart

1. Macrina Wiederkehr, *A Tree Full of Angels: Seeing the Holy in the Ordinary* (San Francisco: HarperSanFrancisco, 1990), 57.

2. William Shannon, *Silence on Fire: Prayer of Awareness* (New York: Crossroad Publishing, 2000), 24.

3. Michael Casey, *Sacred Reading: The Ancient Art of Lectio Divina* (Liguori, MO: Liguori Publications, 1996), 62.

4. Thelma Hall, *Too Deep for Words: Rediscovering Lectio Divina* (New York: Paulist Press, 1988), 41.

5. Maria Lichtmann, *The Teacher's Way* (New York & Mahwah, NJ: Paulist Press, 2005), 87.

6. Wiederkehr, 57.

7. Thelma Hall, *Too Deep for Words: Rediscovering Lectio Divina* (New York: Paulist Press, 1988), 42.

8. Ibid., 43.

9. John Forman, personal correspondence to coauthor Sr. Lucy Wynkoop, 2006. Forman uses repetitive cello practice to describe composer Matthew Dallman's thoughts on the progression of increasing artistic facility. Forman's analogy was adapted to *lectio.*

10. Esther de Waal, *A Life-Giving Way: A Commentary on the Rule of St. Benedict* (Collegeville, MN: Liturgical Press, 1995), 159.

11. Casey, 61.

12. Ibid., 55.

Chapter 6. Contemplative Awakening and Awareness

1. William Shannon, *Silence on Fire: Prayer of Awareness* (New York: Crossroad Publishing, 2000), 32.

2. Walter J. Burghardt, "Contemplation: A Long Loving Look at the Real," *Church* 14 (Winter 1989): 15.

3. Thomas Merton, *New Seeds of Contemplation* (New York: New Directions, 1961), 1.

4. Ibid., 3.

5. William Shannon, *Silence on Fire: Prayer of Awareness* (New York: Crossroad Publishing, 2000), 32.

6. Shannon, 11.

7. Frank Tuoti, *Why Not Be a Mystic?* (New York: Crossroad, 1995), 83.

8. Merton's *New Seeds of Contemplation* further explains his idea of the true and false self.

9. Merton, 41.

10. Ibid., 38.

11. Teresa of Avila, *The Interior Castle*, trans. Kieran Kavanaugh, OCD, and Otilio Rodriguez, OCD (New York: Paulist Press, 1979).

12. Wendy Farley, "The Transformation of Faith: Contemplation as Resistance in a Postmodern Age," *Memphis Theological Seminary Journal*, vol. 36, no. 2 (1998): 49.

13. Dorothee Soelle, *The Silent Cry: Mysticism and Resistance* (Minneapolis, MN: Augsburg Fortress Press, 2001), 283.

14. Burghardt, 16.

15. Merton, 65.

16. Shannon, 24.

17. William Johnston, ed., *The Cloud of Unknowing* (New York: Image Books Doubleday, 1973).

18. Thomas Keating, "The Method of Centering Prayer," pamphlet (Butler, NJ: Contemplative Outreach, Ltd., 2005), 1.

19. *The Cloud of Unknowing*, 56.

20. A few authors and their books on centering prayer include Thomas Keating, *Open Mind, Open Heart: The Contemplative Dimension of the Gospel* and *Manifesting God: Intimacy with God*; M. Basil Pennington, *Centering Prayer: Renewing an Ancient Christian Prayer Form* and *Finding Grace at the Center: The Beginning of Centering Prayer*; and Stephanie Iachetta, *The Daily Reader in Contemplative Living: Excerpts from the Works of Thomas Keating*.

21. For further information on the purgative way, see Michael Downey, ed., *The New Dictionary of Catholic Spirituality* (Collegeville, MN: The Liturgical Press, 1993), 800–802.

22. Ibid., 529–31, for further information on the illuminative way.

23. Ibid., 987–88, for further information on the unitive way.

Chapter 7. Lectio as Scripture Study, Prayer, and Living

1. Joan Chittister, *Illuminated Life: Monastic Wisdom for Seekers of Light* (Maryknoll, NY: Orbis Books, 2000), 76.

2. Walter Brueggemann, *The Message of the Psalms: A Theological Commentary* (Minneapolis, MN: Augsburg, 1984), 19.

3. Irene Nowell, "The Psalms: Living Water of Our Lives," *Tjurunga* 56 (May 1999): 53.

4. Jean Leclercq, *The Love of Learning and the Desire for God: A Study of Monastic Culture* (New York: Fordham University Press, 1982), 72.

5. Wulstan Mork, *The Benedictine Way* (Petersham, MA: St. Bede's Publications, 1987), 34.

6. Walter Brueggemann, *The Message of the Psalms: A Theological Commentary* (Minneapolis, MN: Augsburg, 1984), 19. Brueggemann speaks of general themes and shows how these themes are used in the psalms that he categorizes as "psalms of orientation" on pages 25–28.

7. Ibid., 19. Brueggemann speaks of general themes and shows how these themes are used in the psalms that he categorizes as "psalms of disorientation" on pages 51–54.

8. Brueggemann, 19. Brueggemann speaks of general themes and shows how these themes are used in the psalms that he categorizes as "psalms of new orientation" on pages 123–25.

9. Luke Dysinger, "Accepting the Embrace of God: The Ancient Art of *Lectio Divina*," *Valerymo Benedictine* 1 (1990): 4. Also see Norvene Vest, *Gathered in the Word* (Nashville: Upper Room, 1996).

10. Patricia Brown, *Paths to Prayer: Finding Your Own Way to the Presence of God* (San Francisco: Jossey-Bass, 2003), 60.

Chapter 8. Shortened Lectio for Busy Days

1. Joyce Rupp, *The Cup of Our Life: A Guide for Spiritual Growth* (Notre Dame, IN: Ave Maria Press, 1997), 15.

2. Sister Dorothy Robinson, OSB, from St. Placid Priory devised this simple process of *lectio divina*; it has been used in The Priory Spirituality Center in Lacey, Washington.

Chapter 9. Journaling, Making Art, and Praying with Art with Lectio

1. Robert Benson. *Living Prayer* (New York: Jeremy P. Tarcher, 1998), 175.

2. Macrina Wiederkehr, *A Tree Full of Angels: Seeing the Holy in the Ordinary* (San Francisco: HarperSanFrancisco, 1990), 58.

3. Jerome Kodell, "*Lectio Divina* and the Prayer Journal," *Review for Religious* 39 (1980): 587.

4. Rachel M. Srubas, *Oblation: Meditations on St. Benedict's Rule* (Brewster, MA: Paraclete Press, 2006), 7

5. John of Damascus, *On the Divine Images* (Crestwood, NY: St. Vladimir's Seminary Press, 1997), 20.

6. See Web site of Timothy Smith *Soli Deo Gloria*, Glossary, copyright © 1996: http://jan.ucc.nau.edu/~tas3/glossary.html.

7. See Barbara Newman, ed., *Voice of the Living Light: Hildegard of Bingen and Her World* (Berkeley: University of California Press, 1998), for further information on Hildegard of Bingen's life.

8. Hildegard of Bingen, *Hildegard of Bingen's Symphonia*, trans. Barbara Newman (Ithaca: Cornell University, 1988), 143.

9. Frederic Brussat and Mary Ann Brussat, "Movies," *Spirituality and Health*, Sept/Oct (2006), 86. These sentences are often said to have been quoted in a speech by Nelson Mandela. The source is *Return to Love* by Marianne Williamson, New York: HarperCollins, 1992.

10. Frederic Brussat, and Mary Ann Brussat, "The Ten Most Spiritually Literate Films of 1998," *Spirituality and Health*, Winter (1999): 6.

11. Frederic Brussat and Mary Ann Brussat, "The Ten Most Spiritually Literate Films of 2004," *Spirituality and Health*, April (2005): 64.

12. For additional ways of praying with the body, see Carla Desola, *Movement Meditations: To the Songs of Taize* (videocassette, Paulist Press); J. Michael Sparough and Betsey Beckman, *Full Body Blessing: Praying with Movement* (audiocassette, St. Anthony Messenger Press); and Michael Sparough, *The Body at Prayer II* (audiocassette, St. Anthony Messenger Press).

Chapter 10. The Transformational Value of Lectio

1. John Cassian, *Conferences,* trans. Colm Luibeid, Classics of Western Spirituality (New York: Paulist Press, 1985), 129.

2. Christopher Bamford, "Thinking as Prayer: *Lectio Divina,*" *Parabola* (Fall 2006): 17.

3. Ibid., 15.

4. Joan Chittister, *The Illuminated Life: Monastic Wisdom for Seekers of Light* (Maryknoll, NY: Orbis Books, 2000), 32.

5. Gerald May, *The Awakened Heart* (San Francisco: HarperSanFrancisco, 1993), 158.

6. Timothy Fry, ed., *RB 1980* (Collegeville, MN: The Liturgical Press, 1981), 506–7.

7. Chittister, 38.

8. Michael Casey, "Saint Benedict's Approach to Prayer," *Cistercian Studies* 15 (1980): 342.

9. Jacqueline Bascobert Kelm, *Appreciative Living: The Principles of Appreciative Inquiry in Personal Life* (Wake Forest, NC: Venet Publishers, 2005), 47.

10. Stephen Kiesling, "Wired for Compassion," *Spirituality & Health* (Sept/Oct 2006): 50.

11. Joan Chittister, *Wisdom Distilled from the Daily: Living the Rule of St. Benedict Today* (San Francisco: HarperSanFrancisco, 1991), 101.

12. Ibid.

13. Basil Pennington, *Lectio Divina: Renewing the Ancient Practice of Praying the Scriptures* (New York: Crossroad Classic, 1998), 89.

14. William Shannon, *Silence on Fire: Prayer of Awareness* (New York: Crossroad Publishing, 2000), 25.

15. *The Sayings of the Desert Fathers: The Alphabetical Collection,* trans. Benedicta Ward (Kalamazoo, MI: Cistercian Publications, Inc., 1975), 103.

16. Loyse Morard, "*Lectio Divina*: The Place of Sacred Scripture in Our Lives," *Benedictine* LII:1 (Summer 1999): 17.

17. Gregory the Great, *Life and Miracles of St. Benedict (Book Two of the Dialogues)*, trans. Odo J. Zimmermann and Benedict R. Avery (Collegeville, MN: no date given), 71.

18. *Julian of Norwich: Showings*, trans. Edmund Colledge, OSA, and James Walsh, SJ, Classics of Western Spirituality (New York: Paulist Press, 1977). For more information on using a *lectio divina* approach to praying with illness, see Mary C. Earle, *Broken Body, Healing Spirit: Lectio Divina and Living with Illness* (New York: Morehouse Publishing, 2003).

Bibliography

Bamford, Christopher. "Thinking as Prayer: *Lectio Divina.*" *Parabola* (Fall 2006): 10–18.

Benson, Robert. *Living Prayer.* New York: Jeremy P. Tarcher, 1998.

Brown, Patricia. *Paths to Prayer: Finding Your Own Way to the Presence of God.* San Francisco: Jossey-Bass, 2003.

Brueggemann, Walter. *The Message of the Psalms: A Theological Commentary.* Minneapolis, MN: Augsburg, 1984.

Brussat, Frederic, and Mary Ann Brussat. "Movies." *Spirituality & Health* (Sept/Oct 2006): 86.

———. "The Ten Most Spiritually Literate Films of 2004." *Spirituality & Health* (April 2005): 64–68.

———. "The Ten Most Spiritually Literate Films of 1998." *Spirituality & Health* (Winter 1999): 6–7.

Bryant, Fred. *Savoring: A New Model of Positive Experience.* Mahwah, NJ: Lawrence Erlbaum Associates, 2006.

Burghardt, Walter J. "Contemplation: A Long Loving Look at the Real." *Church* 14 (Winter 1989): 14–18.

Casey, Michael. *A Guide to Living in the Truth: Saint Benedict's Teaching on Humility.* Liguori, MO: Liguori Publications, 2001.

———. *Sacred Reading: The Ancient Art of Lectio Divina.* Liguori, MO: Liguori Publications, 1996.

———. "Saint Benedict's Approach to Prayer." *Cistercian Studies* 15 (1980): 327–43.

Cassian, John. *Conferences.* Translated by Colm Luibeid. New York: Paulist Press, 1985.

Chittister, Joan. *The Illuminated Life: Monastic Wisdom for Seekers of Light.* Maryknoll, NY: Orbis Books, 2000.

———. *Wisdom Distilled from the Daily.* San Francisco: HarperSanFrancisco, 1991.

De Waal, Esther. *A Life-Giving Way: A Commentary on the Rule of St. Benedict.* Collegeville, MN: Liturgical Press, 1995.

Dowling, Dolores. "*Lectio,* Our Daily Nourishment for Discernment." *Benedictines* (1996): 6–18.

Downey, Michael, ed. *The New Dictionary of Catholic Spirituality.* Collegeville, MN: The Liturgical Press, 1993.

Dysinger, Luke. "Accepting the Embrace of God: The Ancient Art of *Lectio Divina.*" *Valerymo Benedictine* 1 (1990): 1–4.

Earle, Mary C. *Broken Body, Healing Spirit: Lectio Divina and Living with Illness.* New York: Morehouse Publishing, 2003.

Farley, Wendy. "The Transformation of Faith: Contemplation as Resistance in a Postmodern Age." *Memphis Theological Seminary Journal,* vol. 36, no. 2 (1998): 39–50.

Farmer, William R., ed. *The International Bible Commentary.* Collegeville, MN: The Liturgical Press, 1998.

Freedman, David Noel, Gary A. Herion, and John David Pleins., eds. *The Anchor Bible Dictionary,* Volume 1 A–C; 3 H–J. New York: Doubleday, 1992.

Fry, Timothy, ed. *RB 1980.* Collegeville, MN: The Liturgical Press, 1981.

Gregory the Great. *Life and Miracles of St. Benedict,* Book 2 of the *Dialogues.* Translated by Odo J. Zimmermann and Benedict R. Avery. Collegeville, MN: no date given.

Guigo II. *The Ladder of Monks and Twelve Meditations.* Translated by Edmund Colledge and James Walsh. Kalamazoo, MI: Cistercian Publications, 1979.

Hall, Thelma. *Too Deep for Words: Rediscovering Lectio Divina.* New York: Paulist Press, 1988.

Herbaux, Marie-Francois. "Formation in *Lectio Divina.*" *Cistercian Studies* 18 (1982): 127–40.

Hildegard of Bingen. *Hildegard of Bingen's Symphonia.* Translated by Barbara Newman. Ithaca, NY: Cornell University, 1988.

John of Damascus. *On the Divine Images.* Crestwood, NY: St. Vladimir's Seminary Press, 1997.

Johnston, William, ed. *The Cloud of Unknowing*. New York: Image Books Doubleday, 1973.

Keating, Thomas. *Invitation to Love: The Way of Christian Contemplation*. New York: Continuum, 1996.

———. *Open Mind, Open Heart: The Contemplative Dimension of the Gospel*. Twentieth Anniversary Edition. New York: Continuum, 2006.

———. "The Method of Centering Prayer," pamphlet. Butler, NJ: Contemplative Outreach, Ltd., 2005.

Kelm, Jacqueline Bascobert. *Appreciative Living: The Principles of Appreciative Inquiry in Personal Life*. Wake Forest, NC: Venet Publishers, 2005.

Kiesling, Stephen. "Wired for Compassion." *Spirituality & Health* (Sept/Oct 2006): 48–51.

Kodell, Jerome. "*Lectio Divina* and the Prayer Journal." *Review for Religious* 39 (1980): 582–91.

Leclercq, Jean. *The Love of Learning and the Desire for God: A Study of Monastic Culture*. New York: Fordham University Press, 1982.

Lichtmann, Maria. *The Teacher's Way*. New York & Mahwah, NJ: Paulist Press, 2005.

Martin, James. *Becoming Who You Are: Insights on the True Self from Merton and Other Saints*. New York & Mahwah, NJ: Paulist Press, 2006.

May, Gerald. *The Awakened Heart*. San Francisco: HarperSanFrancisco, 1993.

Merton, Thomas. *New Seeds of Contemplation*. New York: New Directions, 1961.

Morard, Loyse. "*Lectio Divina*: The Place of Sacred Scripture in Our Lives." *Benedictine* LII:1 (Summer 1999): 14–21.

Mork, Wulstan. *The Benedictine Way*. Petersham, MA: St. Bede's Publications, 1987.

Newman, Barbara, ed. *Voice of the Living Light: Hildegard of Bingen and Her World*. Berkeley, CA: University of California Press, 1998.

Nowell, Irene. "The Psalms: Living Water of Our Lives." *Tjurunga* 56 (May 1999): 53–66.

Pachomius. *Pachomian Koinonia*, vol. 2. Translated by Armand Veilleux. Kalamazoo, MI: Cistercian Publications, 1981.

Pearmain, Elisa Davy. *Doorways to the Soul: 52 Wisdom Tales from Around the World*. Cleveland, OH: Pilgrim Press, 1998.

Pennington, Basil. *Lectio Divina: Renewing the Ancient Practice of Praying the Scriptures*. New York: Crossroad Classic, 1998.

Rupp, Joyce. *The Cup of Our Life: A Guide for Spiritual Growth*. Notre Dame, IN: Ave Maria Press, 1997.

Shannon, William. *Silence on Fire: Prayer of Awareness*. New York: Crossroad, 2000.

Soelle, Dorothee. *The Silent Cry: Mysticism and Resistance*. Minneapolis, MN: Augsburg Fortress Press, 2001.

Srubas, Rachel M. *Oblation: Meditations on St. Benedict's Rule*. Brewster, MA: Paraclete Press, 2006.

Teresa of Avila. *The Interior Castle*. Translation by Kieran Kavanaugh, OCD, and Otilio Rodriguez, OCD. New York: Paulist Press, 1979.

Tuoti, Frank. *Why Not Be a Mystic?* New York: Crossroad, 1995.

Vest, Norvene. *Gathered in the Word*. Nashville: Upper Room, 1996.

Ward, Benedicta, Trans. *The Sayings of the Desert Fathers: The Alphabetical Collection*. Kalamazoo, MI: Cistercian Publications, Inc., 1975.

Wathen, Ambrose. "Monastic Lectio: Some Clues from Terminology." *Monastic Studies* 12 (1976): 207–15.

Wiederkehr, Macrina. *A Tree Full of Angels: Seeing the Holy in the Ordinary*. San Francisco: HarperSanFrancisco, 1990.

For Further Reading

Arico, Carl. *A Taste of Silence.* New York: Continuum, 1997.

Bianchi, Enzo, and James W. Zona. *Praying the Word.* Kalamazoo, MI: Cistercian Publications, 1998.

Bly, Robert, ed. *The Soul Is Here For Its Own Joy: Sacred Poems from Many Cultures.* Hopewell, NJ: The Ecco Press, 1991.

Casey, Michael. *Toward God: The Ancient Wisdom of Western Prayer.* Liguori, MO: Triumph Books, 1995.

Dumm, Demetrius. *Flowers in the Desert: A Spirituality of the Bible.* New York: Paulist Press, 1987.

Feiss, Hugh. *Essential Monastic Wisdom: Writings on the Contemplative Life.* San Francisco: HarperSanFrancisco, 1999.

Guenther, Margaret. *The Practice of Prayer.* Cambridge, MA: Cowley Publications, 1998.

Ladinsky, Daniel. *Love Poems from God: Twelve Sacred Voices from the East and West.* New York: Penguin Compass, 2002.

Magrassi, Mariano. *Praying the Bible: An Introduction to Lectio Divina.* Collegeville, MN: Liturgical Press, 1998.

Masini, Mario. *Lectio Divina: An Ancient Prayer That Is Ever New.* New York: Alba House, 1998.

Merton, Thomas. *Opening the Bible.* Collegeville, MN: The Liturgical Press, 1986.

Miller, Robert J. *Falling into Faith. Lectio Divina* Series, Cycle C. Franklin, WI: Sheed and Ward, 2000.

Mulholland, Jr., M. Robert, *Shaped by the Word.* Revised Edition. Nashville, TN: The Upper Room Books, 2000.

Salvail, Ghislaine. *At the Crossroads of Scriptures: An Introduction to Lectio Divina.* Boston: Pauline Books and Media, 1996.

Shannon, William H. *Seeking the Face of God.* New York: Crossroad, 1988.

Stewart, Columba. *Prayer and Community: The Benedictine Tradition.* Maryknoll, NY: Orbis Books, 1998.

Swenson, Don. "*Lectio Divina*: From Abiding in the Word to This Word Abiding in Us." *Benedictines* Winter (1997).

Vermeiren, Korneel. *Praying with Benedict: Prayer in the Rule of St. Benedict.* Translated by Richard Yeo. Kalamazoo, MI: Cistercian Publications, 1999.

Vest, Norvene. *No Moment Too Small: Rhythms of Silence Prayer & Holy Reading.* Kalamazoo, MI: Cistercian Publications, 1994.

Advance Praise for Lectio Divina

"I highly recommend Paintner and Wynkoop's *Lectio Divina*. While many books laud the value of integrating *lectio* into our lives—some providing the briefest of explanations—this is the only source I am aware of that provides both the tradition and development of *lectio divina* along with contemporary expressions of *lectio* in practice. This book has grown out of years of practice and of mentoring others to cultivate ways of *lectio divina*, which deepens the contemplative stance toward life. *Lectio* has been the heart and gut of monastic practice for centuries; the Spirit invites all of God's people to partake of this ancient way with God."

—**Sr. Laura Swan, OSB**, author of
The Forgotten Desert Mothers (Paulist Press)

"*Lectio Divina* is above all a *practical* book. It is rooted in the authors' own practice and in the experience of those for whom they provide spiritual direction. It gives practical advice for readers who wish to deepen their life with God on the basis of prayerful reading of the Bible, and of the other ways in which God's word reaches us. Those who listen with their hearts to these authors' words will be deepened in their spiritual practice."

—**Fr. Hugh Feiss, OSB**, Monastery of the Ascension

"With the rising interest in the art of *lectio divina*, Christine Valters Paintner and Lucy Wynkoop have created a work of great promise. In this superb resource the ancient wisdom and the poetry of the *lectio* process shines forth. This is a praiseworthy offering."

—**Macrina Wiederkehr, OSB,** author of
Seven Sacred Pauses and *A Tree Full of Angels*

"Christine Valters Paintner and Lucy Wynkoop offer a way of practicing *lectio divina* that is inviting, accessible, and practical. Their deep confidence in this way of prayer, and the clarity and wisdom with which they beckon the reader, spring from their own lived experience. With its singular combination of insights for daily life and prayer, as well as suggestions for practice, this book will prove helpful to both the novice and to those who teach this way of prayer."

—**Rev. Mary C. Earle,** associate faculty of the
Episcopal Seminary of the Southwest in Austin and
author of *Broken Body, Healing Spirit: Lectio Divina
and Living with Illness*

"Wynkoop and Paintner's *Lectio Divina* is a lovely book, with a gentle, lyrical style that reveals *lectio*'s aim in the authors' tone as well as words. In their hands, *lectio* takes shape as a transforming power, combining the great aspiration to love and be loved by God, with full acceptance of ourselves as we are. I especially enjoy the way Wynkoop and Paintner integrate the prayer of *lectio* with the senses, describing its wisdom as basking and luxuriating in God's presence, and offering specific suggestions for integrating art, poetry, images, music, and the body into a *lectio* practice. *Lectio Divina* is an act of consecration—the lifting up of our lives and souls to God."

—**Dr. Norvene Vest, OblSB**

"Paintner and Wynkoop have given us a true wisdom book in *Lectio Divina*: it is both practical and inspiring, and it shows us the way to good. The authors have a good command of scripture, spirituality, and the wonders of the human person. Their wisdom springs from experience and is presented with clarity. The book draws the reader in and makes him or her want more."

—Sr. Irene Nowell, OSB

"Sister Lucy Wynkoop and Dr. Christine Valters Paintner's *Lectio Divina* provides an immensely practical guidebook for discerning the voices of God and for being with the vicissitudes of contemporary life. This text's divination of the word of God—from the Hebrew *midrash*, to the Christian desert mothers and fathers, to St. Benedict—is a manual inviting us not only to hear anew, but also to feel, see, write, touch, and be moved by Sophia's whisperings....The authors' invitation to embody that 'still, small voice' makes *lectio* accessible as a practice for discernment. And such practices of contemplative education are critically needed."

—Sarah Williams, PhD, professor of feminist theory
Evergreen State University